Baby Steps

Baby Steps

EXERCISES FOR BABY'S FIRST YEAR OF LIFE

Susan Fox

Berkley Books, New York

This book is an original publication of The Berkley Publishing Group.

BABY STEPS: EXERCISES FOR BABY'S FIRST YEAR OF LIFE

A Berkley Book / published by arrangement with the author

PRINTING HISTORY
Berkley trade paperback edition / November 1999

The Penguin Putnam Inc. World Wide Web site address is
http://www.penguinputnam.com

ISBN: 0-425-17057-8

BERKLEY®
Berkley Books are published by The Berkley Publishing Group,
a division of Penguin Putnam Inc.,
375 Hudson Street, New York, New York 10014.
BERKLEY and the "B" design are trademarks belonging to Penguin Putnam Inc.

PRINTED IN THE UNITED STATES OF AMERICA
10 9 8 7 6 5 4 3 2 1

To our Father in heaven for the precious gift of life.

To the babies—you are our immortality, the children of our hearts and souls that we may share with you the best we have to give.

To my daughter, Kate—who I love more than all the stars in the sky, more than all the colors in the rainbow, more than all the raindrops that fall from the clouds.

Acknowledgments

This book took more than five years to write and would never have been possible without the patience, generosity, and willingness to help of many people.

Thank you to the following:

Gifted therapists Wendy Lind, O.T.R., and Linda Rutter, R.P.T., who offered so much expertise, experience, and time and who believed in this book;

Outstanding N.D.T. instructors, including the Bobaths, Jutta Sternberg, and Gay Girolami, who provided precious knowledge and learning experiences;

Gloria Coronado, who transformed this book with her fine mind and her wonderful analytical and organizational skills through several rewritings. This book could never have been done without her;

Julie Chi—you were there with whole-hearted commitment, excellent skills at the computer and digital camera, and worked long evenings to meet deadlines. I am so grateful and blessed to be able to work with you;

Special thanks to my agent, Margot Maley Hutchison, who took a chance on a first-time author; and Alison Blake, who provided excellent, sensitive, and creative editing to help the book find a home. You are the best;

A big cheer to Patty King at Penguin Putnam, a true champion who went above and beyond;

And to my daughter, Katie, who gave up a lot of time with her mom;

To Sandy Senter, Mike and Janet Porter, Diane Fogdall, Doreen

Acknowledgments

Twohy, Pam Bissell, Barbara Grewell, Marie Eng, Eve Riskin, Cathy and Patrick Chase—my heartfelt gratitude and appreciation for all you've given;

And finally, a standing ovation to the parents and babies who were photographed and shared themselves.

Contents

Contents

Contents

Contents

Baby's Workout List

Baby Steps

Introduction

The next few years will be an adventure. Your baby, so helpless right now, will learn to crawl, walk, talk, and explore the world. Before you know it, your infant will be a young child heading off to school.

The fun and simple exercises in *Baby Steps*, based on my twenty years of experience as a neurodevelopmental therapist, can prepare your baby for that big day. These exercises look like "child's play," but they're carefully designed to help your baby reach his or her full physical *and* mental potential.

You may be asking, "Does my baby *really* need to exercise?" The answer is "Yes!" Babies who practice physical skills improve their strength, balance, coordination, visual abilities, dexterity, and even listening skills and memory— and infants who master these basic skills will be stronger, better coordinated, more self-confident, and possibly even smarter.

In fact, exercise during your baby's first year of life can be more important than exercise in later years. That's because your baby's brain, far from being fully formed at birth, is changing every day. All of the brain cells are in place at birth, but the connections *between* cells are still forming—and new research shows that this brain "wiring" process depends largely on a baby's experiences from birth to age three. When you give your baby opportunities to move and explore, you're building brain pathways that will translate into academic skills and physical talents later in life.

Furthermore, many babies (even those who appear to be developing right on schedule) may have problems with coordination, balance, or other critical skills needed for crawling, walking, and other developmental stages. With the help of *Baby Steps*, you'll be able to spot problems early and work on them *before* they block your baby's progress. That's important, because babies who don't master critical developmental stages may lack the foundations for later skills.

While *Baby Steps* is designed to enhance your baby's skills, it's also designed to be fun for your baby—and everyone in the family can join in. Even young brothers and sisters can participate, with supervision from mom or dad. Furthermore, you can rest assured that these exercises are safe. As a pediatric therapist, I've been careful to design exercises that won't stress your baby's developing joints and muscles. I've also arranged the exercises so that every new skill is taught in the correct sequence, just when your baby is ready to learn it. (That's important, because there's a "window of opportunity" for learning most skills. Try too early, and your baby isn't ready. Try too late, and a skill that might have come naturally will be difficult for your baby to master.) In addition, I've broken the exercises down into small steps, to make them easy for you and your baby.

Introduction

SKILLS YOUR BABY CAN DEVELOP
BY EXERCISING

These skills are the building blocks of successful development. As your baby grows, each skill will build on previously learned skills.

VESTIBULAR FUNCTION: This inner-ear system tells your baby when she is moving, and in what direction (critical for all skills requiring balance, and for preventing falls and injuries).

GROSS MOTOR SKILLS: The "big muscle" skills, including arm, shoulder, hip, and leg movements, are important for strength, balance, stability, and coordination.

FINE MOTOR SKILLS: Finger dexterity and other small muscle movements are critical for writing, drawing, painting, playing musical instruments, and other activities requiring small, coordinated movements.

HEARING: Listening skills will help your baby learn to differentiate sounds and voices, imitate sounds, follow directions, learn new words, and develop memory skills (critical for speech, language development, and learning).

VISUAL SKILLS: Focusing and "tracking" objects with the eyes are skills your baby needs to learn about his or her environment, achieve good eye-hand coordination, and succeed in academic skills such as reading, writing, and spelling.

SENSORY SKILLS: Sense of touch and temperature and "body awareness" are needed for baby to develop a sense of self and others, learn spatial concepts, and develop mental "patterns" for learning and remembering how to move; they are also necessary for developing skills such as eating, toothbrushing, potty training, and writing.

COGNITIVE SKILLS: Short-term and long-term memory, organization, attention span, remembering and mentally arranging information, problem solving, and following directions are necessary for success in school and life.

If your baby is a newborn, start with the "calm and comfort" exercises in chapter 1. These exercises, safe and fun for even the youngest baby, will help your infant learn to relax and enjoy an exciting but sometimes frightening world, and can help your baby learn how to nurse correctly, and even "poop" and pass gas with ease. They also will help your baby learn to integrate sights, sounds, and touch, an important step in early learning.

As your baby grows, exercises such as "Hug the Ball" and "Rock 'n' Roll" will help him or her develop skills including rolling over, sitting up, crawling, and walking. Additional exercises will help develop social and play skills, visual and spatial perception, thinking and memory skills, body awareness, listening, and prelanguage abilities. And if you're the parent of a premature infant or a special-needs baby, you'll find special activities to help your baby reach his or her potential.

Because I know how hectic life with a new baby can be, I've designed activities that are simple, require only about 2 to 5 minutes each, and don't use any fancy equipment. So take a break and enjoy doing these exercises with your baby. You'll both have a great time—and you'll be giving your new son or daughter a head start on life!

Introduction

PRECAUTIONS

🐾 If your baby has any health problems that might make exercising risky, consult your physician before continuing.

🐾 Although some sections describe specific physical conditions, this book is not intended to be used as a diagnostic aid. If you have concerns about your baby's development, consult your physician.

🐾 If your baby has significant developmental problems, this book can supplement, but cannot replace, a professional assessment and individual treatment program.

Chapter One

Calm and Comfort

Congratulations—your baby is finally here! The long wait is over, and you're at the beginning of one of life's most exciting, fun, frustrating, scary, thrilling, and rewarding experiences: the experience of being a parent.

Right now, you're probably a little bit frightened by your new responsibility, and by this fragile and demanding little bundle you've brought home. Don't worry—that's a normal reaction. Pretty soon, you'll be a natural when it comes to feeding, diapering, and comforting your new baby.

The first step in getting to know your baby is to understand baby talk. The pitch, intensity, and type of her cry will tell you if she's hungry, in pain, bored, sleepy, or asking for a change or a cuddle. Soon you'll be able to decipher this code, and life will get easier for you *and* your baby.

Meanwhile, your baby is learning, too. She's discovering how to suck, how to swallow, and how to cope with the world beyond the protection of the womb. Sounds, sights, temperature, and movement are bombarding your baby's newly exposed body. Easily upset and tired, she may not know how to calm down. In the hospital, your baby may have had blood drawn, shots, restraints, or medical procedures that made her fearful of touch.

In addition, natural processes such as digestion, including gas and bowel movements, may overwhelm your baby at first. Before she was born, mom's body handled all the hard work, so these are new experiences for her. Eating and bowel movements involve your baby's entire body, and both processes take some time to master.

During this exciting but stressful time in your baby's life, you can help her by finding the most comfortable ways to hold, feed, change, and calm her. The exercises in this first chapter will aid in this "getting acquainted" process, by helping your baby develop the skills she needs to eat, sleep, and tolerate new sensations and changes in position.

BEFORE WE START:
Tips for Dealing with Fussy Babies

Does your baby have a fussy period each day? It's not surprising that newborns sometimes become overwhelmed; after all, being "on the outside" is a big change from the peace and safety of being in the womb. Your newborn's fussy times can be stressful for everyone, so it's best to prevent them when you can.

Notice when your baby's fussy times usually occur, and try

to be at home then. Also, pay attention to the clues your baby offers about what calms him down. Some babies, for instance, love movement, and find rocking and being walked very enjoyable. Sound is very soothing to some babies, while others love being cuddled and held closely. Explore which kind of input your baby prefers—sights, sounds, touch, or movement—and provide that type of comfort and support during his cranky times.

Slow, firm touch and gentle movements are especially important in calming a newborn baby. Swaddling comforts many babies, because this feels most like the snug enclosure of the womb.

At first, your baby is likely to have trouble making the transition from waking to sleeping. After all, he's spent nine months in total darkness, lulled by his mother's heartbeat—the perfect environment for dozing off and waking peacefully. Now, suddenly, he's in a bright, noisy environment that probably seems like Grand Central Station! It'll be easier for him to nap if you keep his environment as quiet and restful as possible, and avoid bright lights and sudden movements. Also, if your baby often falls asleep in his stroller, consider getting a car seat that converts to a stroller. This will allow you to move your sleeping baby from the stroller to the car seat, and back to the stroller, without disturbing a precious nap.

If your baby frequently fusses, try to intervene *before* he gets really upset. Anticipate his hunger when he wakes up, and have bottle or breast ready. Be on the lookout for signs that he's tired *before* he becomes so upset that it's hard for him to calm down. When he wakes up, get to him promptly, because at this stage he doesn't know how to wait or how to comfort himself.

Your baby will be most comfortable when he's dressed in soft cotton or velour clothes with the tags removed. Avoid fussy, frilly, itchy clothing, overalls with straps, or clothing that must be pulled over your baby's head. Like you, your baby is more relaxed if he's dressed casually.

THE STARTLE REFLEX

Changes in position, including being picked up or put down, may cause your baby's arms and head to fly backward, behind his shoulders. This "startle" is scary and uncomfortable for most babies, and can cause your baby's shoulder and back muscles to tense up. Here are some simple techniques to reduce the frequency of the startle reflex.

- Provide support to your baby's head and shoulders, encircling his shoulders and keeping his head, arms, and shoulders well forward.
- Touch your baby firmly, and then *wait several seconds* before lifting or moving him.
- When you pick your baby up or put him down, make sure you move him slowly and smoothly.
- Avoid pulling on your baby's arms or legs when diapering, dressing, or lifting him.
- Avoid bouncing or shaking your baby, or standing him up.
- Avoid pushing against your baby's arms, hands, legs, or feet.

TIME TO GET STARTED!

It's important and easy to help your baby learn new skills as you go through the everyday activities of diapering, dressing, feeding, playing, and cuddling. I've started with exercises that will calm and comfort your baby, integrate her startle reflex, and help her grow accustomed to touch and other sensations. Additional exercises will help your baby master the art of nursing, either from the breast or from a bottle.

These exercises, and the play exercises later in the chapter, will also promote sensory-motor and visual development, and help your baby learn body awareness by beginning to identify her hands, mouth, tummy, and other body parts. In addition, they'll make her more eager to use her body to touch, see, and explore the world around her.

The activities in this chapter will allow your baby to practice holding her head over the center (midline) of her body, in preparation for more advanced skills such as sitting and walking. With her head centered, your baby will experience the feeling of symmetry, and she'll able to initiate her own movements—her first step toward independence—while she's safely supported and stabilized. Several of the exercises in this section will help your baby learn to focus her eyes (a skill called "optical righting"), which is the first step in keeping her head centered.

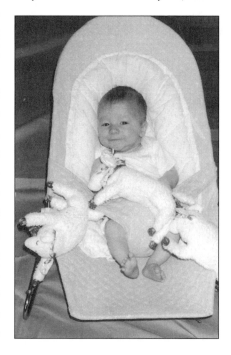

These exercises can be done by parents, nannies, and grandparents, and sometimes even older brothers and sisters. They're a wonderful way for your entire family to bond with your new arrival. And while they're designed to develop your baby's skills, they're also designed to be fun—so enjoy!

Calm and Comfort

Baby's Skills to Start

For most babies, the following skills will be present at birth. Some babies, however, may need some time to develop these skills.

- I can grasp your finger when you place it in my hand
- When you stroke my cheek, I turn my head toward you
- I can put my fist in my mouth
- My knees, ankles, and elbows are bent close to my body (rolled towels or swaddling can be used to keep baby's arms and legs close to the body)
- I look/hold a gaze for at least 5 seconds (some babies will only be able to focus for a few seconds at first)
- I can stay awake for at least a 10-minute feeding (some babies feed more slowly and tire easily)

EXERCISES

Baby Cradle

SKILLS TO BUILD

- Keeping head in midline
- Using both eyes to focus on a parent's face, promoting bonding
- Overcoming startle reflex
- Developing stability in shoulders by learning to keep both arms forward and together

EXERCISE

- Place your baby on your lap, face up, with his hips and knees bent.
- Cradle your baby's head, shoulders, and arms, providing support to ensure that his head is in midline (centered) and that his chin is touching his chest.
- Your baby's arms should be forward and in front of his shoulders.
- Keep your baby's bottom elevated, with his feet touching your chest.
- Gently move your legs from side to side about one inch at a time, paying special attention to your baby's toler-

ance to movement. If your baby stiffens, startles, or fusses, slow the movement down or stop.

NOTE: This exercise can help your baby learn to keep his head forward and his chin tucked, which helps build good suck and swallow reflexes and prevents choking.

NOTE: It's important to keep your legs together and your knees touching, so that your baby's head does not fall backward.

Face to Face

SKILLS TO BUILD

- Holding head in midline
- Improved shoulder stability
- Inhibiting of startle reflex
- Eye–hand coordination

EXERCISE

- Sit on the floor, against a wall, or in a chair, with your knees and hips bent.
- Place your baby in your lap, on her back and facing you, keeping her head in midline and her hips bent. Your knees should be touching each other.
- Place your hands on your baby's elbows and shoulders to provide support and stability as needed.
- Encourage your baby to look at you. Give her hand a kiss. Sometimes it's fun to do this exercise with a soft toy in your mouth (as shown) to entertain your baby.

Got You—Reaching Forward

- Sit on the floor in the same position as Face to Face: your back against the wall and your knees bent, providing shoulder support to your baby as needed.
- Help your baby reach forward by moving her arm to touch your face or mouth.
- Encourage your baby to move her hand back to touch your face again.

NOTE: Gradually provide less support to your baby's arms as she is able to take over and develops increased shoulder and arm stability.

Hold My Hand

SKILLS TO BUILD
- Fine motor skills in hands
- Enjoyment of touch
- Opening hands (decreases the influence of grasp reflex and prepares your baby to release and hold toys)
- Hand dexterity, in preparation for crawling

EXERCISE 1
- Hold your baby on your lap with her head and back well supported and her head in midline (centered).
- Gently open your baby's hand and place it palm down on top of your left palm.
- With your right hand, gently push down on

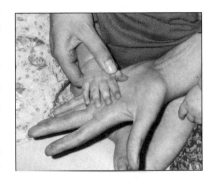

the top of your baby's hand. At the same time, gently push up with your left palm.
- Alternate hands.

EXERCISE II
- Practice the same exercise with your baby's thumb turned up, so that she experiences a "handshake" with open hands.

TIP: If your baby doesn't like holding her hand fully opened, rub her partially opened hand.

Rock-a-Baby

SKILLS TO BUILD
- Relaxation
- Tolerating movement without startling

EQUIPMENT
- Non-stretch quilt or blanket approximately 40 inches x 36 inches or larger.

EXERCISE
- Place the blanket on the floor, and fold the sides of the blanket toward the middle.
- Place your baby snugly in the center of the blanket.
- Firmly gather the fabric on the top and bottom ends of the  blanket, at your baby's head and feet.
- Lift your baby, keeping his head well forward and his upper arms and legs inside the blanket.

- Gently rock your baby forward and backward and/or side to side.

NOTE: Once your baby has fallen asleep, the blanket can be used to ease him into his crib without waking. This position minimizes startle and provides stability similar to that experienced in the womb.

Go Gas/Help Me Poop

SKILLS TO BUILD
- Relaxing spasm or tightness in tummy muscles to move gas or poop through bowel area
- Lifting legs/hips to provide stability for tummy muscles to squeeze

EXERCISE I

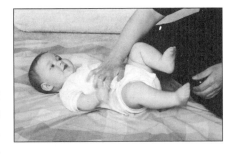

- Place your baby on his back, either on the floor or in your lap.
- Using the flat part of your palm (not your fingers), gently knead your baby's tummy muscles from side to side. (Do not do this if your baby's tummy stiffens or if he cries.)
- Gently massage for 3 minutes.

EXERCISE II
- Using the same position as in Exercise I, bend your baby's legs at the hips and spread his legs two to three inches.
- Gently push your baby's legs against his tummy. Provide support at his knees or feet.

- Roll your baby from side to side if he seems to enjoy the movement.
- Continue this exercise for 3 to 5 minutes.

EXERCISE III

- Place your baby on his tummy, positioned across your lap.
- Gently stroke your baby's back from neck to bottom, patting intermittently. This position supports your baby's tummy and helps gas rise to surface.

TIP: Patting from the top down helps move muscle contractions down.

Diapersize

Diapering is an excellent opportunity for your baby to experience movement and develop balance. This exercise allows your baby to experience the feeling of having one leg bent while the other leg is straightened, preparing her for walking.

SKILLS TO BUILD

- Keeping head in midline, chin tucked, and head forward
- Keeping arms forward and adjusting to weight shifting, which will reduce your baby's startle reflex and enhance early balance skills
- Increased muscle strength

EQUIPMENT

- Blanket or small pillow (2 to 3 inches thick) for head support

EXERCISE

- Place a folded blanket on your baby's changing table.
- Place your baby on her back, with her head and shoulders forward.
- Make sure your baby's head is centered.
- While diapering your baby, lift each leg separately, rather than lifting both legs at the same time. Be sure to make your movements slow and gentle. After lifting and bending one leg, slowly let the leg drop, and then lift and bend the other leg.

 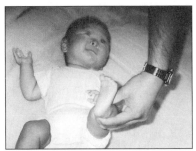

Tummy Tilt

SKILLS TO BUILD

- Being on tummy and exploring, lifting the head
- Increasing neck and back strength, extension, and body alignment
- Bringing head from side to midline and keeping head centered
- Keeping arms and head forward, which reduces startle

Calm and Comfort

EQUIPMENT

- A soft musical toy or bright patterned fabric

EXERCISE I

- Place your baby on his tummy, across your lap. Place the toy or fabric where your baby can look at it and reach for it.
- Lift the leg under your baby's head about 3 inches so your baby is at a slight incline.
- Make sure your baby's arms and elbows are in front of his shoulders.
- Provide stability by pushing down gently on your baby's back and bottom, to encourage him to lift his head while keeping his head in midline.

TIP: When lifting your leg, raise the leg that is closer to your baby's head so that your baby is at an incline, with his head higher than his hips. You can practice this position while dressing your baby.

EXERCISE II

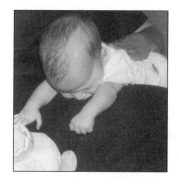

- Reduce *incline* as your baby learns to lift his head on his own.
- Stroke your baby's back from upper back to bottom, to encourage your baby to lift his head in midline with his arms forward.

Here is a progress chart you can use to follow your baby's motor development. If your baby is a preemie or developmentally delayed, some or all of these skills will appear later than they are shown on the chart.

EARLY MOTOR SKILLS

Week	2	4	6	8	10	12	14	16	18	20
Keeps head in midline when sitting in infant seat with round head support insert	👣	👣	👣	👣	👣	👣	👣	👣	👣	👣
Moves legs separately		👣	👣	👣	👣	👣	👣	👣	👣	👣
On tummy, turns head from midline to side	👣	👣	👣	👣	👣	👣	👣	👣	👣	👣
Focuses on object with both eyes		👣	👣	👣	👣	👣	👣	👣	👣	👣
Puts hands together		👣	👣	👣	👣	👣	👣	👣	👣	👣
Opens fisted hand, moves fingers		👣	👣	👣	👣	👣	👣	👣	👣	👣
Turns head from side to midline			👣	👣	👣	👣	👣	👣	👣	👣

IMPORTANT: Every baby develops differently. These skills can emerge as late as the last time listed on the chart, and still be well within normal limits.

LEARNING TO FEED

Eating isn't as easy as it looks! Many parents worry when their babies don't immediately know how to breast- or bottle-feed, but this isn't an unusual problem. I remember being surprised when my baby and I had to work together on this skill. It took us several days to become comfortable with nursing, and you may have the same experience.

Because your baby is accustomed to being fed through the umbilical cord, she's not used to being touched near or in her mouth. At first, she may find this contact surprising. In addition, it may take some time for your baby to develop the skills she needs to breast- or bottle-feed successfully.

Feeding is a combination of coordination, strength, and endurance. In order to eat, your baby must be able to coordinate sucking and swallowing. She also has to learn to close her mouth, and to use her lips and cheeks to form a seal. In addition, she has to learn the feeling of tucking her chin and holding her head forward.

The activities in this section will address all of these important skills. If your baby is experiencing some frustrations with feeding, practicing these activities every day can help make mealtime easier and more successful.

A FEW THINGS TO REMEMBER
WHEN FEEDING YOUR BABY

- Support your baby's head, making sure that it's well forward and centered during feeding, to prevent choking.
- If your baby has trouble sucking, explore various feeding positions on your lap or in an infant seat.
- If your baby startles easily, swaddling him before feeding may help. The warmth and contact remind your baby of the womb, and provide stability.

- New babies eat only a few ounces at a time and tire easily. Over time, your baby will be able to eat larger amounts as his tummy grows and he can stay awake for longer periods. For the baby who tires easily, offer a bottle at least every couple of hours.
- Try various nipples and bottles. Some nipples are designed for premature infants and require only minimal suction. Many babies nurse well with Nuk or Playtex nursers, which are most like mom's nipple.
- Avoid squeezing milk into your baby's mouth. If you're worried that your baby isn't eating enough, use an eyedropper at the end of the feeding to express tiny amounts of milk at a time.
- If your baby is prone to vomiting or spitting up, be sure to keep him upright for at least a few minutes after feeding him.

THE BREAST-FED BABY

Breast-feeding can be a challenge, and it often takes mothers and babies a few days to get the hang of it. Be patient with yourself and your infant! Explore different positions that will allow you both to become comfortable with the process.

A baby who is highly sensitive may not like the skin-to-skin contact of breast-feeding. Work on this sensitivity with exercises that teach your baby to enjoy touch around his face and mouth. Exercises that teach your baby to form a good seal using his lips and cheeks will also help him breast-feed successfully. Most babies, including those who were premature or had health problems at birth, can learn to breast-feed with minimal help.

If you are breast-feeding your baby and are having trouble, a number of resources are available. These include lactation consultants (usually available through the obstetrical department of a hospital), your pediatrician, or your local chapter of the La Leche League.

THE BOTTLE-FED BABY

If your baby is bottle-fed, be sure to position her with her head forward, to prevent choking. Either hold her in your arms while feeding her, or place her in an infant seat with her head well supported. If she's a fussy eater, try coaxing her to eat for longer periods by stroking her cheek, or by undressing her and holding her skin-to-skin with you. She's also likely to enjoy her mealtimes more if you rock her gently while feeding her.

Some babies tire easily during feeding. These babies may not take in enough nourishment because they can't achieve a sustained suck-and-swallow pattern. Sometimes they have trouble keeping their lips closed, and milk leaks from their mouths. The exercises in this section will help teach your baby to gain control of the muscles in her jaw and lips, which is necessary for a good suck-and-swallow pattern.

On the following page is a progress chart you can use to follow your baby's feeding skills. If your baby is a preemie or developmentally delayed, some or all of these skills will appear later than they are shown on the chart.

Early Feeding Skills

Week	1	2	3	4	5	6	7	8
Coordinates breathing, sucking, and swallowing	🍼	🍼	🍼	🍼	🍼	🍼	🍼	🍼
Sucks for 5 minutes	🍼	🍼	🍼	🍼	🍼	🍼	🍼	🍼
Swallows with closed lips	🍼	🍼	🍼	🍼	🍼	🍼	🍼	🍼
Sucks hands		🍼	🍼	🍼	🍼	🍼	🍼	🍼
Feeds for 10 to 15 minutes		🍼	🍼	🍼	🍼	🍼	🍼	🍼
Closes mouth with tongue behind lips			🍼	🍼	🍼	🍼	🍼	🍼
Gets hands to mouth			🍼	🍼	🍼	🍼	🍼	🍼
Breathes through nose if not congested			🍼	🍼	🍼	🍼	🍼	
Smacks lips								🍼

IMPORTANT: Every baby develops differently. These skills can emerge as late as the last time listed on the chart, and still be well within normal limits.

LEARNING AND PLAYING

You can spend a fortune on toys for your baby—but you don't need to. For the first few months, your baby needs only a few toys to help him learn to look, listen, explore, touch, and entertain and comfort himself.

Swings are ideal at this age, because they position and support your baby so he can see the world around him. Use a head support for the first 1 to 2 months, until baby can hold his head up well. (I recommend buying a battery-operated swing rather than a wind-up swing, because it'll give you more free time—a precious commodity!) Also, buy toys that will encourage your baby to look and to follow movement. For instance, toys with contrasting colors, such as red or black and white, will help your baby learn to focus his eyes. (Newborns can't distinguish colors well, but they *can* distinguish between light and dark.)

Your baby will prefer toys with obvious facial features. Also, your baby first learns about his own body by becoming aware of his feet and hands, so give him wrist rattles or sock toys (for instance, Playskool™ Infant Sox) that provide visual or sound input. Your baby can play with these toys in his seat or swing, which will foster independence in an enjoyable way. Because he can't grasp toys at this stage unless they're placed in his hand, he'll favor toys that can be attached to his swing or seat, or to his wrists or ankles.

Now is the time to start reading to your baby, too. Of course, he can't follow a story yet—but he can learn to associate books with fun, and the quiet time you spend together in the rocking chair looking at picture books will help him unwind after a noisy, ever-changing day. In addition, reading to your baby will help him learn to pay attention, will build visual skills such as focusing and eye tracking, and will encourage him to hold his head up so he can see the pictures. Books with pictures of faces will help your baby develop "body concept" as he begins to recognize eyes, noses, and mouths in the pictures he sees. As I've mentioned, newborns can't distinguish colors well, so choose books with black-and-white photos and art. Select books with pictures of single faces or objects, rather than "busy" drawings or cartoons that will confuse your baby.

Best Books for This Age

- Black-and-white pattern books
- Cloth or plastic picture books or cards of faces and shapes
- Simple picture books with one object per page
- Books with pictures of people

TOY/EQUIPMENT	SKILL

Face Cards, Black and White

1. Promotes visual awareness and focusing
2. Helps baby detect contrast of light and dark
3. Teaches baby to control head in midline
4. Teaches baby to turn head from side to midline.
5. Promotes integrated "asymmetrical tonic neck reflex": when baby turns head to side in order to see pictures, the opposite arm will bend and flex, helping to initiate reaching

Links to Hang Toys

1. Helps baby look at and touch toys; provides visual and tactile stimulation
2. If toys are placed midline on links, helps baby learn to bring hands and eyes to midline
3. Promotes integrated "asymmetrical tonic neck reflex" (see above)
4. Allows child to learn about objects by touch

Black-and-White Cloth Book

1. Promotes head lifting and looking
2. Encourages baby to turn head from side to midline
3. Provides practice in visual focus and tracking

4. Helps baby explore touch and looking
5. Provides early exposure to language

Baby Swing

1. Helps baby learn to focus eyes
2. Provides movement in space
3. Teaches autonomy and the self-confidence to play and interact without being held
4. Develops eye-hand coordination as baby plays with toys

Note: Use a head support until your baby has the head control necessary to hold his body symmetrically.

Playskool™ Infant Sox or Velcro Wrist Band

1. Fosters visual awareness and eye focus
2. Promotes awareness of feet—the beginning of body awareness
3. Teaches baby to look to midline
4. Promotes head turning from side to midline
5. Encourages voluntary leg movement

Ocean Dreamer™

1. Promotes visual attention skills
2. Promotes listening skills
3. Teaches baby to turn to sound
4. Develops head control by encouraging baby to look
5. Helps baby to fall asleep, using rhythmical sounds

Balloon Bop

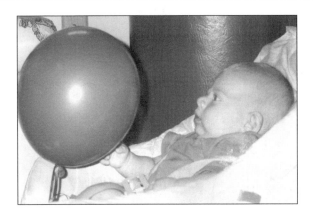

SKILLS TO BUILD

- Looking to midline
- Visual focus and eye-tracking skills
- Integrated startle reflex
- Improved eye-hand coordination

EXERCISE

- Place your baby in her infant seat.
- Tie a helium balloon at the base of the seat harness. Make sure the balloon is at your baby's shoulder height, and close enough that if she reaches forward (1 to 2 inches), she can touch the balloon.

NOTE: Constantly supervise your baby while playing this game, so that if the balloon pops, your baby won't put it in her mouth and swallow it! Mylar balloons are best because they are less likely to pop.

Here is a chart you can use to follow you baby's learning skills. If your baby is a preemie or developmentally delayed, some or all of these skills will appear later than they are shown on the chart.

EARLY LEARNING SKILLS

Week	1	2	3	4	5	6	7	8	9	10
Sits in bouncer with head support	👣	👣	👣	👣	👣	👣	👣	👣	👣	👣
Snuggles, enjoys being held	👣	👣	👣	👣	👣	👣	👣	👣	👣	👣
Looks at hands and at brightly contrasting colors			👣	👣	👣	👣	👣	👣	👣	👣
Explores/touches self (face and hands)			👣	👣	👣	👣	👣	👣	👣	👣
Strokes/pats blanket			👣	👣	👣	👣	👣	👣	👣	👣
Attempts to reach for a toy						👣	👣	👣	👣	👣
Looks toward a sound						👣	👣	👣	👣	👣
Shakes hand with wrist rattle							👣	👣	👣	👣
Anticipates breast or bottle by looking or turning toward it						👣	👣	👣	👣	👣
Calms when gently rocked in swing or baby seat. Enjoys movement in swing						👣	👣	👣	👣	👣

IMPORTANT: Every baby develops differently. These skills can emerge as late as the last time listed on the chart, and still be well within normal limits.

Calm and Comfort

BABY'S ACCOMPLISHMENTS

When your baby has mastered the exercises in this chapter, he'll be able to show off these new skills:

- I turn to watch faces, or to respond to changes in light or sound

- I can get my hand to my mouth

- In a car seat or infant seat, I am able to keep my head centered with head support

- When I'm upset, I am able to calm down when I'm held or rocked

- When I'm on my tummy, I can lift and turn my head to one side

- Sometimes I will lift one leg and straighten the other

"CAN YOU TELL ME WHY...?"
Answers to Questions Parents Often Ask

My baby's head is always turned to one side. Why?
All babies' heads occasionally fall to one side or the other. However, some babies' heads *always* tilt to the left or the right. This is a common condition called *torticollis,* caused by a muscle imbalance. Sometimes torticollis occurs because of a baby's position before birth. The problem often resolves itself by the time a baby is 6 months old, and by 3 months you should see significant improvement. If your baby's torticollis doesn't improve, consult your physician and ask for a referral to a pediatric therapist. Without intervention, your baby could be at risk for scoliosis in later life.

To help overcome torticollis, try these techniques:

• Using a rolled towel for head support, keep your baby's head and neck propped in alignment. This lets your baby experience the feeling of symmetry, and gives her practice in holding her head centered.
• Encourage your baby to turn and lift her head toward her less dominant side by approaching her from that side.
• Reposition the crib so that your baby uses her weaker side to turn.
• Place your baby on her side to play for some time each day.

My baby doesn't like his car seat or stroller. What can I do?
Check out the size and angle of your car seat. If your baby is fussy, try a specially designed car seat for infants aged up to 6 months. Smaller infants benefit from a car seat insert that provides greater stability. Experiment with the angle of the car seat, and make

sure it isn't too far forward. Provide support for your baby's head, using a car seat insert or small, rolled-up towel if necessary.

If your baby fusses in his stroller, make sure it's well padded. Use a pacifier with a clip to comfort your baby, and a shade or window screening to protect his eyes. If possible, purchase a reversed-handle stroller. Many babies enjoy hearing and seeing the person pushing them in the stroller.

Also, try using the car seat or stroller in the house. Gradually expose your baby to the car seat, initially using it for about three minutes at a time. Play music for him, or set him in front of a baby video. Try holding the car seat on your lap, or setting it on the sofa next to you. Kiss and praise your baby when he's sitting in the seat.

My baby cries a lot when she's not being held, and I can't hold her all day long!

Many infants, even those who are only a few days old, enjoy an infant bouncing seat. Front packs or slings also keep babies happy while freeing parents' hands. Many babies like spending time in a baby swing, but do use a head support at first.

My baby cries when I undress or bathe him.

Some babies are sensitive to temperature changes. Here are some ideas for making bathing and dressing less traumatic:

- Place a warm, wet washcloth over your baby's chest and tummy so he isn't completely uncovered while being bathed.
- Dress your baby in a two-piece outfit, so he can gradually become accustomed to being undressed.
- Bathe him only from the waist down, keeping his T-shirt on.

- Bunch up sleeves and pants legs, and push your baby's limbs through slowly, instead of pulling his arms and legs into his clothing.
- Dress your baby slowly on your lap, and keep his arms and head well forward, to reduce his startle reflex.
- Take a bath with your baby. Your presence will reassure him.

My baby isn't sleeping more than 2 hours at a time, night or day. I'm exhausted. What can I do?

Some babies take a long time to develop a deep sleeping pattern. It's miserable, for your baby *and* for you. Some people advocate letting your baby cry up to 15 minutes, while other people advocate bringing your baby in bed with you. There is no right or wrong answer in this situation, so use your own judgment. And be patient, because less than half of all babies sleep through the night before they are over a year old.

I am feeling angry at my baby's demands, and sad that this is not what I expected. I have no time to do anything.

Most parents are surprised and a little shocked at the time a baby takes. It's normal to be frustrated when you're tired, stressed, and have trouble completing tasks you used to do effortlessly. If it's any comfort, remember that as your baby grows older, you'll gradually regain your freedom.

If possible, do something special for yourself each day: buy a magazine, indulge in a bubble bath, or rent an old movie you've always wanted to see. Just because you've had a baby, that doesn't mean your *own* needs aren't important! If you can afford it, hire a baby-sitter or a nanny to spell you; if not, ask family members if they can help. (And remind dad that it's *his* baby, too! Encourage him to take your baby for a walk or a drive every night, so you'll have at least a few minutes of peace and quiet.)

My baby sucks for only a few minutes, then tires and falls asleep.

Newborns are sleepy for the first few days, but after that, babies usually feed for at least 10 to 15 minutes at a time. Consult your physician's nurse, a lactation consultant, or La Leche League if feeding difficulties continue for more than a week. Also, try rubbing your baby's head to keep him awake, or undress him so he's not too warm. Rocking him and playing music may help, too.

What about a pacifier or a bottle?

Many women who breast-feed feel strongly opposed to bottles or pacifiers, but there's no reason to feel guilty if you use them. I nursed my baby until she was nearly 2 years of age—but I also gave her a bottle beginning when she was 4 days old, because I occasionally wanted to go out for a few hours and didn't want her to be hungry. Also, bottle-feeding gave my husband a chance to participate in her care. As for pacifiers, my daughter sometimes used one for comfort, usually when I wasn't around. I say, do whatever works for you. I don't believe there is a right or wrong to pacifiers or bottles.

If you are breast-feeding, do introduce your baby to a bottle by the time he's 6 weeks old; otherwise, he may refuse to use one. Give him a bottle about 3 times a week, and he'll be able to switch from breast to bottle easily.

My baby seems especially fussy, and I can't get her to calm down! She startles easily at loud noises and cries more than other babies I've seen. What am I doing wrong?

Some babies are more sensitive to outside stimulation than others. This is normal, and you don't need to be alarmed. Do try to provide her with only one type of sensory input (vision, touch, movement, sound) at a time, so she doesn't become overwhelmed.

My baby isn't gaining weight, and I really want to nurse. What can I do?
The S&N nurser often works well. La Leche League or a lactation consultant can provide this equipment, which uses formula or breast milk. Basically, a tiny tube is attached to the mother's nipple; the other end of the tube is connected to a small plastic pouch that fits between mom's breasts and contains milk or formula that can be expressed into the baby's mouth slowly, as she learns to suck.

I have successfully transitioned several babies and mothers from the S&N to independent breast-feeding as their babies learned to suck.

My baby cries and fusses anytime anything touches his mouth. This is getting in the way of feeding, and I'm worried he won't eat enough. Is there a way to help him get over this?
Several simple techniques can help a baby with an especially sensitive mouth. If your baby is so sensitive that he won't even suck his thumb, try this: holding your baby's hand open, palm down, against your palm, apply gentle pressure. This contact will help your baby get used to touch in a less sensitive spot.

Some babies have a very strong "rooting" reflex (a reflex that causes babies to turn their heads when they're touched on their cheeks), and this can frighten your baby at first. When diapering your baby, gently touch his lips and cheeks. Gradually, he'll get used to this feeling and enjoy using his lips, mouth, and tongue.

What can I do if my baby doesn't close her mouth all the way?
Here's a simple exercise to help your baby learn to

close her mouth. Place your baby on your lap in a sitting position, making sure her head is centered and she's well supported. Use your index finger to bring your baby's top lip down so that both of her lips are together. Provide support to her lower jaw and lip as needed to keep her mouth closed. Smack your lips together and encourage your baby to imitate you, giving her time to respond and cuing her by stroking her top lip if necessary. Don't do this exercise if your baby is congested.

My baby's tongue sticks out of his mouth, and it seems to keep him from being able to eat very well. He drools all the time. Is this something I should be worried about?

Some babies need time to learn how to suck and swallow, and keeping the tongue inside the mouth is part of this process. If your baby is having trouble with this skill, try holding him on your lap with his back and head well supported. Keep his head in midline and his chin down so he can't arch. When your baby's tongue is in front of his lips, firmly push down on the middle of his tongue with your index finger. Gently stroke his top lip to give him the feeling of keeping his lips together. Support his lower jaw to give him stability and allow him to breathe and swallow with his mouth closed.

NOTE: Don't do these exercises if your baby has a cold or is ill, because he may not be able to breathe with his mouth closed when his nose is congested. If your baby has a strong tongue thrust, it may be several months before he closes his mouth independently.

We received a baby bouncing chair at my baby shower, but my daughter screams whenever I put her in it. I'd like to find something for her to sit in, but I don't know what else would be safe. What can I do?

Try a baby swing. Make sure you support your baby's head with an infant head support, a rolled towel, or a receiving blanket, and always start on the lowest swing setting. (At first, your baby may prefer to sit in the swing without moving.) Singing or speaking quietly to your baby while she swings will encourage her to interact with you, and keep her head in midline while it's being supported.

Many babies who don't like bouncing chairs or swings enjoy going for rides in their strollers—even in the house! Consider buying your baby the stroller/car seat combo, which I mentioned earlier.

Swings and bouncing chairs help your baby experience feelings of support and symmetry, but she can also do this while lying down. Place your baby on her side, using a small pillow to keep her from rolling. You can give her extra help by stabilizing her shoulder and hip to keep her arms forward and hips bent. Then place an interesting toy in front of your baby, within reach of her hand. Encouraging her to watch or touch the toy will help her experience symmetry (the feeling of both sides of her body working together), and will stimulate her senses of touch and vision.

Calm and Comfort

PARENTS' STORIES *

MARISSA

I hated bath time, and so did Marissa. Every time I put her in the tub, she sobbed, and I felt like crying with her. Then I tried a simple trick: I heated a bath towel in the dryer and wrapped Marissa in it, uncovering and bathing only one part of her body at a time. After a few weeks she became less sensitive, and now she loves taking a bath in her "birthday suit!"

JEFFERSON

Jefferson wasn't interested in eating. He would nurse for a few minutes, then fall asleep—even though my breasts were still full of milk. I was frustrated, and I worried that he wasn't getting enough nourishment.

To encourage Jefferson to nurse longer, I sang to him and stroked his cheek. I also undressed him, so he could feel my skin next to his. He loved rocking, so I always rocked him when I fed him. It worked: he gradually started feeding for longer and longer amounts of time, and within a few weeks he was a hearty eater.

* Children's names have been changed to protect their privacy.

I Can Hold My Head Up

There's so much for your baby and you to discover now!
One thing you're discovering, no doubt,
is that your clean, tidy house is a
thing of the past. If you're like
most parents, your home is
cluttered with diaper
boxes, toys, baby swings,
pacifiers, and bottles. My
advice? Don't worry
about it. Disarray is okay,
because your baby's needs
take priority.

At this stage you're better
able to handle those needs,
because you're becoming an expert at
baby language. You can read subtle cues, and can hear the
differece between "I'm hungry" and "I'm tired" cries. Your
baby is learning language from you, too: even though he

can't understand your words, he's already starting to identify speech sounds, patterns, and rhythms. (By the way, that's why almost all parents speak in "baby talk." When you exaggerate your speech, it's easier for your baby to distinguish different sounds.)

Your baby is much more alert and aware now, and he's much more a part of your family. In fact, you're probably discovering that he's developing quite a personality. Do you have a quiet baby or a noisy one? A demanding little fellow who likes everything his own way or an easygoing infant? Each week, you'll learn more about what makes your baby "tick," what makes him unique.

In the meantime, you're growing less fearful, and more comfortable and self-assured with your baby. At the same time, your baby is growing more attached to you. He looks deep into your eyes now, and enjoys watching you. In part, that's because he can see better. But in addition, he's beginning to understand that you're somebody who's very important in his life. He recognizes that you're a separate individual, and he may worry and fuss when you leave his side. It's good for him to watch you coming and going, however, because it strengthens his concept of "object permanence"— the knowledge that an object (or mom) still exists even when out of sight. He'll also begin to grasp the concept of "self" and "others."

As your baby grows emotionally, he's also developing physically. At this early stage, it's important for him to develop visual and sensory-motor skills. He practices these skills every day, as he interacts with you and with the world around him. As your baby cuddles with you or plays with his toys, he becomes aware of his body (especially his hands and feet), learns to focus on and grasp for objects, and gains self-confidence and coordination. The exercises in this chapter are designed to foster these skills.

One skill we'll focus on in particular is head control, because it's crucial to your baby's future development.

HEADS UP!

Your baby needs to learn basic skills before she can graduate to more advanced abilities, and the first major skill she'll master is controlling her head. Good head control is a prerequisite for rolling, sitting, crawling, and walking.

At first, your baby's head will fall backward when her body is tilted back. She'll instinctively work on correcting this, and will practice controlling and stabilizing her head an average of 300 to 400 times a day. (And you thought a baby's life was easy!) First, she'll learn to use her eyes to fix on an object. This is called "localization." Once she can focus on an object, she'll learn to use her "optical righting reflex," which causes her head to line up in the direction in which her eyes are looking.

Your baby will develop head control slowly and in tiny increments. First she'll master head control while she's sitting with her head supported, because in that position she doesn't have to deal with the pull of gravity. As she's sitting on your lap or in her infant seat, your baby will practice bringing her head from the side to the center. She'll learn to hold her head in line with her body, not letting it fall backward, forward, or to one side. Holding her head in midline will develop the muscles of her neck and upper back so that she can hold her head up independently. Soon, she'll able to bend her neck to keep her head from falling backward, and lift her head easily if it falls forward.

An important word of caution: Some baby exercise books include exercises at this stage that involve pulling your baby up into a sitting position. DO NOT DO THIS! Pulling your baby up by her arms into a sitting position at this stage can cause her to stiffen at her shoulders, and can result in shoulder dislocation and neck retraction. Usually, children cannot safely be pulled into a sitting position in this way until they are at least 2 years of age.

I Can Hold My Head Up

"Tummy play" is an important part of gaining head control. Because babies are now put to sleep on their backs, it's important for your baby to play on the floor on her tummy when she's awake. In this position, she'll learn to lift her head against gravity, making her shoulders, neck, hips, and back stronger. As she pushes up and becomes more comfortable on her tummy, she'll grow better at balancing and at shifting her weight sideways—skills she'll need later for rolling, sitting, crawling, and walking. Tummy play also helps your baby learn to become more agile, because it teaches her to make smooth, controlled, incremental movements without any fear of falling.

Baby's Skills to Start

Each baby is an individual, and develops at his or her own pace. Be sure your baby has the following basic skills before beginning the exercises in this chapter.

- 🎲 I can look and use my eyes to gaze at you for at least 10 seconds
- 🎲 I look toward lights or bright objects, such as large, colored towels or mobiles
- 🎲 I can turn my head to look from the side to the middle
- 🎲 I enjoy movement or slow rocking, without startling
- 🎲 I can smile
- 🎲 When I'm sitting in my infant seat, I can follow an object moving from the side of my body to the center, and from the center of my body to the side, using both eyes together
- 🎲 I can reach my mouth with my hand
- 🎲 On my tummy, I can lift my head for at least a second
- 🎲 On my tummy, I can bring my head from my left or right side to the middle, and from the middle to either side

EXERCISES

Comfy Tummy Bop

SKILLS TO BUILD

- Lifting head while on tummy
- Reaching forward
- Increased strength of back and tummy muscles, in preparation for rolling and sitting
- Increased shoulder stability and strength, in preparation for crawling

EQUIPMENT

- Bop cushion or towel rolled into a horseshoe shape about 3 inches in diameter
- Toys to watch and touch

EXERCISE

- Place the Bop cushion or horseshoe-shaped towel on the floor. Place your baby on his tummy over the Bop or towel, with his arms forward. (His elbows should be in front of his shoulders.)
- Provide support to your baby's back and bottom if necessary, to help keep his bottom down and stable. Make sure your baby does not flip forward or sideways off the

bop or towel.
- Encourage your baby to lift his head while keeping his head in midline.
- After your baby is able to lift and hold his head in midline, encourage him to reach forward for a toy.

Baby Push-Ups

SKILLS TO BUILD
- Lifting and holding head up in midline
- Increased strength in neck and upper spine
- Supporting weight over forearms, which builds upper body strength

EXERCISE I

- Lie on the floor or a bed in a semi-reclined position, with a pillow under your head. (Your head and shoulders should be off the floor, as though you're doing stomach crunches.)
- Place your baby on her tummy, on your chest.
- Provide support to your baby's back and shoulders so that **her elbows are in front of her shoulders.**
- As your baby is able to maintain the heads-up position, slowly sit up 1–3 inches and then return to your initial position. This encourages your baby to lift her head independently.
- Repeat as needed until your baby can hold her head up while on her tummy.

EXERCISE II

- Lie on the floor in a fully reclined position with your baby on your chest. Make sure **her elbows are in front of her shoulders** to facilitate weight-bearing on her forearms.

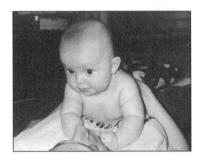

- Encourage your baby to hold her head up independently by playing peek-a-boo. As your baby becomes more stable, gently rock from side to side so she can explore balance.

Tummy Tuck

SKILLS TO BUILD

- Tucking chin when tilted backward, to counterbalance and keep from falling backward
- Bringing upper body forward to keep from falling backward
- Using tummy muscles for stability and balance
- Keeping arms forward and legs bent at knees and hips when tilted backward

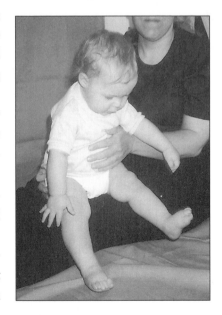

EXERCISE

- Sit on the floor with your back supported. Place your baby on your lap, facing sideways.
- Use one hand to support your baby's tummy and the other to support his back.
- Supporting your baby at the tummy, slowly tilt him backward 1–2 inches. (You'll feel his tummy muscles tighten and contract.)

NOTE: Make sure your baby is tucking his chin. Gradually increase his backward tilt, but only as he learns to keep his head and arms forward and in midline. Head control develops in millimeters.

Baby Sit-Ups

SKILLS TO BUILD

- Keeping head in the middle when tilted sideways
- Balance and equilibrium
- Improved strength of abdominal muscles, which provide support and stability to baby's back for sitting

EQUIPMENT

- Chair with good back support. The chair should allow you to sit with your feet flat on the floor, with a mirror in front of you so you can check your baby's head position and alignment.

EXERCISE

- Sit on the chair with your legs together, and hold your baby

firmly on your lap, facing forward. Check to be sure
your baby's back is straight and well supported by your
body, and her head is centered.

- Wrap one hand around your baby's upper trunk and
  tummy area.
- Use your other hand to stabilize your baby's hip and
  tummy muscles as needed.
- Gently tilt your baby sideways 2–3 inches. Make sure
  she is holding her head up.
- Bring your baby up to midline, providing support as
  needed. Repeat, alternating sides. Make sure your
  baby's head stays in the middle, even when she's tilted
  to the side.

On the following page is a chart you can use to follow
your baby's motor skills. If your baby is a preemie or developmentally delayed, some or all of these skills will appear
later than they are shown on the chart.

BABY'S MOTOR SKILLS

Week	1	2	3	4	5	6	7	8	9	10	11	12	13	14
Keeps head centered with support	👣	👣	👣	👣	👣	👣	👣	👣	👣	👣	👣	👣	👣	👣
Brings hands together			👣	👣	👣	👣	👣	👣	👣	👣	👣	👣	👣	👣
Smiles						👣	👣	👣	👣	👣	👣	👣	👣	👣
Enjoys movement without startling								👣	👣	👣	👣	👣	👣	👣
Tucks chin when tilted backward								👣	👣	👣	👣	👣	👣	👣
Keeps head up while on tummy, plays at least 5 seconds								👣	👣	👣	👣	👣	👣	👣
Bends and straightens legs when lying on back									👣	👣	👣	👣	👣	👣
Takes weight on forearms when placed on tummy										👣	👣	👣	👣	👣
Keeps head centered when weight shifts sideways													👣	👣

IMPORTANT: Every baby develops differently. These skills can emerge as late as the last time listed on the chart, and still be well within normal limits.

LEARNING AND PLAYING

Now that your baby is used to being "on the outside," he's starting to explore and enjoy the world. He can drop objects, rather than just passively holding them. He's getting the idea of object permanence—that is, he's figuring out that Mom, toys, and his own body parts are still there even when he's not looking at them. He'll follow objects with his eyes, such as a moving toy or pictures in a book, and he'll turn his head toward a sound. He's learning to understand words, and starting to make two-syllable sounds and imitate lip-smacking or patting. By now he may also begin fussing when Mom or his caregiver is out of sight.

Your 2-to-4-month-old is exploring language, sounds, and tones of voices. He's also just starting to understand that a word or picture is a symbol for a real object. To help him grasp this concept, read to him from picture books—preferably small (4 to 6 inches) cardboard books that show babies eating, playing, and enjoying other activities. Choose books with real photos of people and objects, rather than cartoons. Books that clip to your baby's stroller or car seat will keep him entertained and help him learn at the same time. In addition to teaching him language skills, they'll help him develop eye–hand coordination when he reaches out to touch the pictures.

When reading to your baby at this stage, use very few words—for instance, "Where's ball?" rather than "Hey, look at the book and see if you can find the ball." Give him plenty of time to respond to your question by directing his eyes to the picture. (This skill is called "eye pointing," and it's the first step toward learning to physically point at an object.) If he doesn't take the hint right away, repeat—"Where's ball?"—and cue him, if necessary, by pointing to or tapping on the picture. Your baby is just learning individual words, so don't string more than two or three together at a time.

BEST BOOKS FOR THE AGE

- Cloth picture books
- Plastic picture books
- Cardboard picture books,
  4–6 inches in size, with baby doing things:

    Baby eating
    Baby playing
    Baby being diapered
    Baby having a bath

- Books with real photos rather than cartoons
- Books that clip to baby's stroller or car seat
- Look for books with only one photo on a page, and with realistic photos or pictures rather than cartoons

Toy/Equipment	Skill

Squeak Duck

1. Turning head to sound
2. Following sound with eyes
3. Listening
4. Anticipation
5. Memory
6. Using eyes and head together

Red Rubber Rings

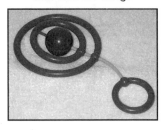

1. Focusing on and following a moving object
2. Grasping and exploring texture
3. Fine motor dexterity

Gund™ Snake

1. Tactile exploration
2. Manual dexterity
3. Grasping skills
4. Tactile discrimination
5. Auditory awareness
6. Visual discrimination skills

Duck Ball in Water

1. Movement in space
2. Cause/effect: eye tracking, following movement
3. Self-confidence/autonomy (baby can make duck move and water splash)

I Can Hold My Head Up

Picture Books

1. Vocabulary skills
2. "Eye pointing"—looking toward an object of interest
3. Concept that words and pictures are symbols of real objects

Soft Doll with Face

1. Object permanence, during doll play with parent (When parent covers doll with a blanket, baby can't see it. When it reappears, baby realizes the doll was still there even when he couldn't see it.)
2. Body awareness of self and others, discovers body parts

Lap Play

SKILLS TO BUILD
- Playing on tummy
- Reaching forward
- Using eyes/head together to develop eye–hand coordination

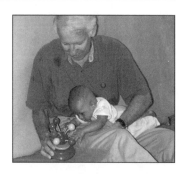

EQUIPMENT
- Piece of brightly printed fabric, soft windup musical toys, cloth books, soft rubber squeak toys, or cloth or patterned ball 3–6 inches inches in diameter

EXERCISE
- Sit comfortably on a chair or the floor with back support.
- Place your baby across your lap. Be sure she's straight, and her head and shoulders are forward.
- Place a toy or fabric in front of your baby so she can easily touch it.
- If your baby is just getting used to being on her tummy, you may lift your legs so your baby is more at an incline.
- Gently help your baby explore the toy or fabric with her hands.
- Play for 1–3 minutes, alternating right and left sides.

NOTE: Be sure to do this on both sides.

NOTE: Always supervise tummy play so that your baby doesn't fall asleep. Physicians recommend that babies sleep on their backs only, to prevent sudden infant death syndrome (SIDS).

On the following page is a chart you can use to follow your baby's learning skills. If your baby is a preemie or developmentally delayed, some or all of these skills will appear later than they are shown on the chart.

BABY'S LEARNING SKILLS

Week	6	8	10	12	14	16	18	20	22	24
Smiles	👣	👣	👣	👣	👣	👣	👣	👣	👣	👣
Gazes at parents 5 seconds	👣	👣	👣	👣	👣	👣	👣	👣	👣	👣
Visually follows objects up/down/across 12 inches in any direction		👣	👣	👣	👣	👣	👣	👣	👣	👣
Produces vowel sounds			👣	👣	👣	👣	👣	👣	👣	👣
Bats at toys			👣	👣	👣	👣	👣	👣	👣	👣
Reaches out arms in request to be picked up or play				👣	👣	👣	👣	👣	👣	👣
Produces 2-syllable sounds "uh-oh"					👣	👣	👣	👣	👣	👣
Fusses when Mom/caretaker is out of sight						👣	👣	👣	👣	👣
Tries to remove a cloth covering face						👣	👣	👣	👣	👣

IMPORTANT: Every baby develops differently. These skills can emerge as late as the last time listed on the chart, and still be well within normal limits.

BABY'S ACCOMPLISHMENTS

When your baby has mastered the exercises in this chapter, he'll have these new abilities:

- I can look at and follow an object 10 to 12 inches from side to side and up and down

- I startle less; my arms are usually forward now

- On my back, I can keep my head centered, and can bend and lift my knees off the floor

- In a supported sitting position, I can hold my head up and centered for at least 10 seconds. I can turn my head to the middle from either my right or left side. I can lift my chin and and tuck it to my chest

- On my tummy, I can lift my head and hold it up for a moment

- I can put my hands together. Both of my hands are open, with my thumbs outside of my palms, at least half the time. For a few seconds, I can hold a toy placed in my hand

"CAN YOU TELL ME WHY...?"
Answers to Questions Parents Often Ask

My husband loves to roughhouse with our son. He throws our baby way up in the air, and the baby screams with delight. But I'm really scared that my husband will drop our baby. Am I just being overprotective?

No, you're being smart. I've treated several babies who suffered serious injuries from falls during such games—one when the family dog got underfoot, and another when the doorbell rang and distracted Dad for just an instant. Your baby and your husband can have just as much fun playing "rough and tumble" games on the floor together, or doing the exercises in this book—and your baby will be much safer.

My baby hates being on her tummy, and cries when I put her on the floor on her stomach. How can I help her?

Some babies simply don't like being on their tummies on the floor. However, many babies will get used to being on their tummies if they lie in that position on Mom's or Dad's lap. Being on her tummy will improve your baby's back extension and alignment in preparation for sitting, and is an important skill for your baby to learn.

My baby is losing all the hair on the back of her head. She has a big bald spot. What should I do?

This is normal, and often happens when a baby lies on her back. When your baby isn't sleeping, put her in other positions, including lying on her side and tummy. (However, do be sure to put your baby to sleep on her back; research strongly indicates that this reduces the chance of sudden infant death syndrome.) Consider buying a baby swing or baby bouncer seat.

My baby doesn't seem to see well. He doesn't look at me, but he looks to light. What can he see?

Most babies don't see well at first. They need to learn to use their eye muscles to focus. For the first 6 weeks, most babies see light and dark contrast only. If this doesn't change by the time your baby is 8 weeks old, see your doctor for a complete evaluation.

My baby seems very strong. He stiffens rigidly and points his feet when bathed. What does this mean?

Between 3 and 4 months, your baby's muscle control improves in his head, neck, and upper back, and he will be able to push. Pushing against gravity prepares your baby to sit and roll, and develops back strength. However, if your baby is arching and stiffening *but is unable to bend*, it's important to discuss this with your physician. Your baby may need help learning to bend and relax his muscles.

My baby doesn't hold toys—he drops them. Should I be concerned?

Don't worry—your baby's doing exactly what he should be doing right now! Believe it or not, toy-dropping is a major milestone in your baby's early development.

Most newborns involuntarily grasp anything you place in their hands. As your baby learns to open his hand and drop toys, usually between 6 and 12 weeks of age, he learns to inhibit this involuntary grasp reflex. He can then learn to grasp objects *voluntarily*—a much more advanced skill than involuntary grasping.

My baby seems too right-handed. One of his hands is always made into a fist. It is even hard to open the hand when I bathe him. Is this a concern?

Babies usually aren't right- or left-handed. If a baby's

hands are always closed and fisted after 2 months of age, it can be a sign of muscle or tone imbalance. Point this out to your physician. To help your baby learn to open his fisted hand, do the "Hold My Hand" exercise in chapter 1. Also, do lots of water play. When your baby is in the tub, slowly pour water over his fist. Open his fisted hand and use it to scoop and release water. In addition, put wrist rattles or bell bracelets on his less-preferred hand.

One side of our baby's head is a little flat. Will this go away? What, if anything, can be done?

This is called skull molding, and it's a fairly common occurrence. Usually it occurs when a baby is frequently placed in one position—for instance, on her back or side. Try positioning your baby on the opposite side from the "dent." Consult your baby's doctor, who may recommend a special plastic helmet that will help the skull to form more evenly as your baby grows. Usually a baby's skull evens out with time and varied positions. Occasionally this problem requires a few visits to a therapist, who can help you work out a corrective program.

My baby is still not sleeping through the night. I'm going crazy! I've just gone back to work and I need to sleep. What do I do?

There are several good books on infants and sleep, including Richard Ferber's *Solve Your Child's Sleep Problems*. Also, try these tricks:

- For a few days, let your husband get up and give the baby a bottle or pat her until she goes back to sleep.
- Make sure your baby doesn't nap for long periods in the late afternoon and early evening.
- Try to keep your baby awake until 10 or 11 P.M.

- Spend extra time with your baby before she goes to sleep, and put articles of clothing you have worn near her so that she can smell your scent for reassurance. Make sure the clothing is placed in such a manner that there's no danger of your baby becoming entangled in it.

I Can Hold My Head Up

PARENTS' STORIES

PARKER

Parker always turned his head to one side. Even with a rounded head support pillow, his head was always tilted toward the right. I noticed this when I diapered him, dressed him, or picked him up from his crib. My pediatrician said he'd outgrow it, but I didn't want to wait, and neither did my husband. We saw a therapist for a few sessions and she gave us suggestions.

First, she recommended that we put rolled-up towels on the right side of Parker's head whenever he was in his car seat or swing. That prevented his head from falling to the right. Also, to encourage him to look toward the left, we turned his crib so that the right side was against the wall. When we approached him in his crib, we'd kiss his left cheek. When we put him in his car seat or infant seat, we always tilted his head to the left. By putting Parker on his left side and then helping him roll to his tummy, we taught him to bring his head from his right side to middle.

It turned out that the pediatrician was right—Parker did outgrow his tendency to lean his head to the right. But I'm certain that the work we did with Parker helped speed up the process!

SARAH

Sarah was forever tossing her toys on the floor. I felt like a retriever, because all I did was "fetch" all day long. No matter what fancy toys I bought her—rattles, plastic keys, balls—she'd toss them, and then whine because she had nothing to play with. Driving was especially stressful, because I couldn't pick up her toys and watch the road at the same time.

I was reassured to learn that her behavior was normal, and that babies drop toys in order to practice opening their hands (which are fisted when they're born). They actually have to master dropping before they can master grasping.

On one wonderful shopping expedition, I discovered wrist bells that attach with Velcro, a toy bar that attaches to Sarah's car seat, and two toys—a squeaky dog and a push-button toy—that can be attached to her seat. Also, a mom in my baby group told me to buy plastic links and elastic at a fabric store. These can be used to attach almost any toy to Sarah's stroller or high chair, or to the car near her car seat. Now Sarah is happy, and I can sit down for more than 2 minutes at a time!

I Can Roll Over

Your baby's seeing more and more of the world each day, and she loves it. She enjoys being carried in a "snuggly" or carry pack, because she wants to be upright and see everything. New people and new places don't scare her the way they once did—in fact, she's hungry for new experiences, as long as she doesn't become overwhelmed.

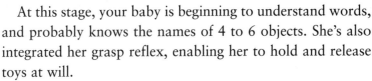

At this stage, your baby is beginning to understand words, and probably knows the names of 4 to 6 objects. She's also integrated her grasp reflex, enabling her to hold and release toys at will.

Your baby still puts everything in her mouth, but now she's about to learn an even more interesting way to explore her universe: by rolling. Her first rolling experience is likely to be a surprising and wonderful accident. Babies frequently roll from their tummies to their backs first, and then, enthralled by this accomplishment, they work at this skill until they can do it with ease.

Rolling teaches your baby to shift her weight from one side of her body to the other, in preparation for sitting, crawling, and walking. It also allows her to explore depth and spatial perception, without any fear of falling.

To master the art of rolling, your baby will first need to learn how to cross the middle of her body with her arms and legs. Many of the exercises in this section will work on crossing midline. They'll also teach your baby to shift her weight and to make the controlled, gradual movements she'll need to master for rolling and later skills.

You'll notice that many of the exercises in this section use the "sidelying" position. That's because it's easiest for your baby to learn how to roll when she's lying on her side. From this position, it's just a short roll to her back or tummy. "Sidelying" also helps a baby develop symmetry, and teaches her to align her hips, back, and shoulders.

I Can Roll Over

Baby's Skills to Start

Your baby should have the following basic skills before beginning the exercises in this chapter:

- 🎲 I can tolerate being on my tummy, either over my parent's lap or on the floor, for at least 1 minute
- 🎲 I can touch my knees or legs while I'm lying on my back
- 🎲 I can reach forward with one or both arms and bat at objects while I'm lying on my back or in a supported sitting position
- 🎲 I can kick my legs, sometimes touching my heels to the floor or to the changing table, when my diaper is being changed
- 🎲 I can make swimming motions when on my tummy

NOTE: These exercises are sequential. It's tempting to hurry each stage, but resist the urge! A good grounding in basic skills will serve your baby best, so take your time at each level.

EXERCISES

Side Roll

SKILLS TO BUILD
- Bringing top arm forward while lying on side
- Opening hand and using fingers to explore a toy
- Playing with two hands together
- Keeping both arms forward while playing in sidelying position
- Improved eye-hand coordination
- Decreased startle reflex

EQUIPMENT
- Any toy that interests your baby

EXERCISE
- Sit in a comfortable chair or on the floor with a firm back support, with your legs forward.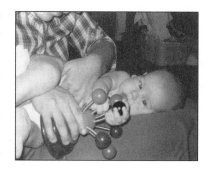
- Place your baby on his side on your lap, his bottom against your chest.
- Place the toy 6 inches from your baby's shoulder, so that his hand touches the toy when his arms are forward.
- Provide stability at your baby's shoulders, if necessary, to keep his arms forward.
- Once your baby can play in this position without falling forward or backward, with both arms forward, bring his top arm down parallel with his side and encourage him to reach forward by himself to touch the toy.
- Place your baby on his other side, and repeat.

Gimme That Toy!

SKILLS TO BUILD
- Keeping head in midline, looking at an object, and reaching forward to touch it
- Eye-hand coordination
- Increased shoulder stability and arm strength

EQUIPMENT
- Soft, textured toy not larger than 3 inches in diameter

EXERCISE
- Place your baby on his back or on your lap, with his knees bent so his bottom is tilted up slightly and his feet rest on your chest. Be sure his head is  in midline, and his head and chin are forward. (Use a small pillow if necessary.)
- Place the toy in your mouth, keeping your face within arm's length of your baby's face.
- Provide support at your baby's shoulder as necessary to encourage him to reach forward to touch the toy. Gradually provide less support at his shoulders, as he learns to reach for and play with the toy independently.
- Encourage your baby to practice reaching with his right arm and left arm separately. As he develops increased shoulder stability, he'll be able to play with toys using both hands together.
- Move the toy slowly from the center to the side so your baby learns to roll.

Rolling to My Tummy

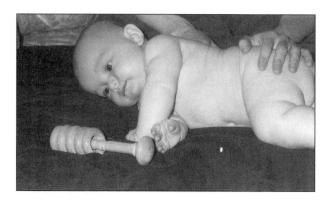

SKILLS TO BUILD
- Reaching forward across midline
- Shifting weight forward
- Rolling from side to tummy
- Eye-hand coordination

EQUIPMENT
- Soft toy

EXERCISE
- Place your baby on the floor on her side, making sure her top leg is bent at the knee.
- Provide stability at her top hip and shoulder to keep her from falling backward or forward.
- Encourage her to bring her top arm forward and reach for a toy.
- Praise your baby for reaching for the toy, and gradually move the toy farther forward, so that the momentum of reaching will propel her onto her tummy.
- Make sure you provide support so that the movement to her tummy is slow rather than fast (which might scare her). Your baby learns best from slow, repeated exercise. Do 3 times on each side.

Found My Foot!

SKILLS TO BUILD

- Lifting one leg
- Reaching across midline
- Shifting weight and balance from side to side
- Experiencing the feeling of having one leg bent, one leg straight, in preparation for walking
- Foot alignment and weight bearing through heel, in practice for standing.

EXERCISE

- Place your baby on her back.
- Bend your baby's leg at the knee and place her foot on the floor with her heel down. Check her foot position to make sure the foot is straight.
- Gently *push down through your baby's knee to the foot*, to give her the feeling of weight through the foot.
- Encourage your baby to play with her other foot. Provide support as necessary. Make sure her head stays in midline as she plays.
- Repeat on opposite side.

Hug and Reach

SKILLS TO BUILD

- Increased strength and stability at shoulders and hips
- Experience of weight shifting, in preparation for rolling

- Increased hip and back extension
- Pushing up while on tummy, in preparation for rolling

EXERCISE

- Lie on the floor with a pillow under your head.
- Place your baby on your chest, on her tummy. Support your baby with one arm across her upper back and

the other across her hips. Use gentle pressure to keep her from raising her bottom.
- Make sure your baby's arms are forward and her weight is supported by her forearms.
- Roll slightly to one side, so that your baby's weight shifts to one side. Check the position of her head; it should stay centered, and not fall to one side or the other.
- Encourage your baby to lift her arm and reach forward. Do 3 times each side.

Rock and Roll

SKILLS TO BUILD

- Increased ability to move around on tummy with head up
- Shifting weight from side to side
- Moving in a circular pattern and reaching for a toy
- Learning to rotate and reach across midline

I Can Roll Over

EQUIPMENT
- Soft quilt
- Any toy your baby enjoys

EXERCISE
- Place your baby on his tummy on the quilt.
- Place a toy at your baby's side, near his elbow.
- Encourage your baby to look at the toy and to reach out to touch it.
- Move the toy 2 inches and and encourage your baby to move in a clockwise pattern. Repeat until he has completed a circle. Then repeat the exercise in a counterclockwise pattern.

Here is a progress chart you can use to follow your baby's motor skills. If your baby is a preemie or developmentally delayed, some or all of these skills will appear later than they are shown on the chart.

BABY'S MOTOR SKILLS

Month	2	2.5	3	3.5	4	4.5	5
SITTING IN INFANT SEAT							
Hands are mostly unfisted (open)				👣	👣	👣	👣
Bends and straightens feet, one leg bent, one straight (bicycle movements)					👣	👣	👣
Holds head in midline well when sitting or lying on back					👣	👣	👣
ON TUMMY							
Lifts chin 2–3 inches with head at 45° angle, keeps head up for 30 seconds				👣	👣	👣	👣
Takes weight on forearms				👣	👣	👣	👣
"Swims" (lifts arms/legs off floor)					👣	👣	👣
Will pivot/push off/turn in a circle						👣	👣

Month	2	2.5	3	3.5	4	4.5	5
ON BACK							
Lifts arm to bat at objects				👣		👣	👣
Touches knees, tummy, and feet					👣	👣	👣
Lifts one leg off the floor while the other leg stays on the floor						👣	👣
Coos, says "Uh-oh"						👣	👣
ON SIDE							
Crosses center of body with an arm to touch a toy	👣	👣	👣	👣	👣	👣	👣
Brings one leg forward to push against the floor with toes	👣	👣	👣	👣	👣	👣	👣

IMPORTANT: Every baby develops differently. These skills can emerge as late as the last time listed on the chart, and still be well within normal limits.

LEARNING AND PLAYING

As your baby learns to roll, she'll explore new skills and refine existing ones. Her head control will improve, and she'll be able to focus clearly and follow you with her eyes as you move around the house or point at pictures in a book. She'll be able to keep her head centered consistently when she looks at toys or pictures, and she'll practice new skills, such as opening her fingers and releasing toys placed in her hand.

In addition, your baby is learning about her own body, and discovering that her hands and feet—those mysterious objects that have fascinated her for weeks—are actually a part of her. She's also developing better hand-eye coordination, depth perception, visual memory (the recollection of objects and faces she's seen), and the beginnings of language skills. In addition, she has a much better concept of "object permanence"—the idea that objects exist even when she can't see them.

Your baby will play by herself for longer periods now without getting fussy, because she's starting to enjoy being independent. Being on her own is more fun for her at this stage, because she's more coordinated and can grasp and bat at toys, move around, and play with her fingers and toes.

Now is a perfect time to share simple books with your baby, as she begins to build a vocabulary. At this stage, she realizes that words are symbols for real things—an exciting revelation! Good books for this age include "peek-a-boo" books with flaps, and books with textures (for instance, the classic *Pat the Bunny*). Books with holes, embedded finger puppets, and squeakers are fun. Your baby will also enjoy books with photos of animals and familiar household and neighborhood objects, and books that show parents and babies doing things together. Play games as you read, to help her learn new words and imitation skills. For instance, when she's looking at a picture, say, "Find the dog!" At this age, your baby will enjoy being an active participant when you read together.

You can also teach your baby language by playing simple games—for instance, the "echo game," in which you repeat the sounds your baby makes. Or play "follow the leader": pat a table, smack your lips, or perform another simple act, then look expectantly at your baby, and say, "Baby's turn!" These games will improve your baby's verbal and listening skills, teach her social skills, and introduce her to the concept of taking turns.

BEST BOOKS FOR THIS AGE:

- Heavy cardboard, or cloth books, plastic books for the tub—these will be chewed and drooled on
- Peek-a-boo books with flaps
- Books with embedded textures
- *Pat the Bunny*
- Books with holes for baby to explore with fingers
- Books with embedded finger puppets
- Books with animal photos (dog, cat)
- Books with squeakers
- Books showing parent and baby doing things together
- Books of familiar objects (food, clothing)

Toys/Equipment	Skills

Rubber Teether or Ring

1. Grasping skills
2. Releasing skills
3. Oral-motor stimulation/desensitization
4. Eye-hand coordination
5. Position in space

Swiss Rattle (4–6 oz.)

1. Spatial orientation (position in space)
2. Spatial relationships
3. Grasping skills
4. Oral/motor stimulation

Bubble Bear

1. Visual motor skills
2. Visual memory
3. Understanding words as symbols of real objects
4. Prelanguage skills—concepts of "up and down," "in and out"
5. Cause-and-effect/anticipation: poke bubbles, they pop

"Action" Books

1. Cause-and-effect: baby can open flaps, play with puppets in book, etc.
2. Spatial relationships: open, close
3. Social interaction
4. Vocabulary skills

I Can Roll Over

5. Object permanence—object still exists even though not visible
6. Visual memory—pictures hidden under flaps

"Wobble Toys"
(placed between your baby and a mirror)

1. Cause-and-effect: baby creates an action
2. Self-awareness: baby enjoys seeing himself in the mirror
3. Spatial orientation
4. Eye-hand coordination

Baby Gym

1. Autonomy: baby learns to play alone happily
2. Self-confidence: baby learns to control the environment
3. Eye-hand coordination
4. Stability at shoulder girdle
5. Cause/effect: when baby bats at object, it moves

Toe Touches

SKILLS TO BUILD

- Lifting legs and touching knees and feet while lying on back
- Experiencing weight shifts, in preparation for sitting and walking

EQUIPMENT

- Rubber or plastic rings, bright striped socks, socks with bells
- Velcro rattles

EXERCISE

- Place your baby on your lap or on the floor with his bottom against your body for support.
- Lift your baby's legs (if he needs help) so that he's able to touch his knees and reach for his toes. Provide support as necessary.
- Place toy on baby's foot or ankle.
- Gradually give less support and encourage your baby to lift, reach, and hold on to his feet independently, and play with toys attached to feet.
- Encourage your baby to roll from side to side.

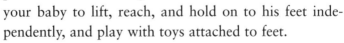

I Can Roll Over

Here is a progress chart you can use to follow your baby's learning skills. If your baby is a preemie or developmentally delayed, some or all of these skills will appear later than they are shown on the chart.

BABY'S LEARNING SKILLS

Month	2.5	3	3.5	4	5	6	7
Stays awake 1–2 hours	👣	👣	👣	👣	👣	👣	
Practices opening hand, fingers	👣	👣	👣	👣	👣	👣	👣
Practices releasing toys placed in hand	👣	👣	👣	👣	👣	👣	
Keeps head in midline when gazing		👣	👣	👣	👣	👣	
Can visually track/follow objects		👣	👣	👣	👣	👣	
Releases toys		👣	👣	👣	👣	👣	
Increased attention span (3 minutes at a time)		👣	👣	👣	👣	👣	
Holds toys for 2–5 seconds				👣	👣	👣	👣
Follows a parent visually				👣	👣	👣	👣
Looks at large-contrast pictures in books, helps turn pages					👣	👣	👣
"Eye points": gazes at familiar objects in the house or in a book					👣	👣	👣
Learns object permanence (something exists even though it's not seen); looks to where an object was last seen when it's dropped				👣	👣	👣	👣
Eye-hand coordination emerges; looks at / reaches for/grasps toys, then lets them drop				👣	👣	👣	👣

IMPORTANT: Every baby develops differently. These skills can emerge as late as the last time listed on the chart, and still be well within normal limits.

BABY'S ACCOMPLISHMENTS

When your baby completes the rolling stage, he'll have these skills:

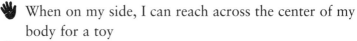

- I can move my head and shoulders separately
- When on my side, I can reach across the center of my body for a toy
- I can bend my knees to my chest
- I can lift my knees off the floor and touch them together, or touch the floor with one leg while the other knee is raised (as though I'm bicycling)
- I can bend my ankles while keeping my legs straight
- I can kick my legs separately, in preparation for walking
- My startle reflex is better integrated. When I'm sitting with support, I can keep my arms forward, and I can tuck my chin when I'm startled or tilted backward
- When I'm on my tummy, I can lift my head while supporting my weight on my forearms
- I can remove a cloth partially covering my face, while I'm lying on my side or back
- When held at my chest and leaned forward, I can bring both arms forward to protect myself
- I can swallow with my mouth closed, when I'm not not congested
- I can roll from my tummy to my back, and from my back to my tummy
- I can look at pictures in a book and direct my eyes to 3 or 4 specific objects (for instance, ball, baby, dog)
- I recognize familiar people—Mom, Dad, Baby-sitter
- I enjoy peek-a-boo

"CAN YOU TELL ME WHY...?"

Answers to Questions Parents Often Ask

My baby rolled when she was 3 weeks old, but she is not doing this now. Is this a problem?

Some babies roll by accident very early on—they just turn their heads and their bodies follow. (Therapists call this "log rolling.") As they develop head control and overcome their startle reflex, they learn to move the upper and lower parts of their bodies separately, and can initiate rolling by using their arms and legs separately. Babies can learn this second, more advanced type of rolling at any age between 4 and 8 months.

My baby can roll from his tummy to his back, but not from his back to his tummy. Why?

Gravity helps your baby roll from his back to his tummy. For your baby to roll from his tummy to his back, he must lift his head, shoulders, and some of his tummy against gravity—in other words, almost 50 percent of his body. Most babies first roll from the back to the tummy, but either way is quite normal. Do help your baby roll from his back to his tummy by practicing the "Rock and Roll" exercise.

When my baby rolls, her arms get stuck underneath her body. Should I be concerned?

Sometimes this happens when a baby first starts to roll, because she doesn't know how to shift her weight from side to side in order to free her arm. If your baby still has difficulty after she's been rolling for at least a month, practice rolling her onto her side and holding her in that position until she brings her arm up. Also try the "Reach and Roll" exercise. If your baby can roll efficiently to one side but not the other, exercise only the side that needs practice.

My baby doesn't like being on his tummy. He cries and still can't lift his head.

First, check out how much head control your baby has. He may need extra support while he's learning to use his neck, shoulder, and tummy muscles to lift. Good exercises include "Lap Play" and "Baby Push-Ups," (chapter 2), and "Hug and Reach" (chapter 3).

Try dressing your baby while holding him over your lap, on his tummy. Also, play with your baby over your lap, or put a rolled towel or wedge pillow under his chest. Eventually he'll graduate to independent tummy play, as he learns to keep his arms forward and push up on them to lift his head.

My baby isn't reaching forward. Is this a problem?

Babies generally begin to reach forward between 8 weeks and 3 months, but there's considerable variation in when a baby is able to do this. To help your baby learn to reach, try the "Baby Cradle"/"Face to Face"/"Got You" exercises in chapter 1. Also, string toys across your baby's infant seat, using plastic links, to encourage her to reach out.

My sister's baby plays with his legs all the time when he's lying on his back on the floor. My son can't seem to lift his legs off the floor, and they are turned out like a frog's. Can I help him?

There are several ways to tackle this problem. First, when you're carrying your baby, don't straddle him over your hip. Instead, hold him so that his legs are together. At night, put him to bed in a bag sleeper, rather than pajamas with separate legs. And when you're diapering your baby, hold his legs together at the knees and let him push against the floor. These techniques will let your baby experience the feeling of keeping his legs together.

Exercises can help as well. Try placing your baby on the floor, with a small pillow behind his head if necessary, and lifting his legs together so that he can easily touch his toes. Provide support for him and hold his legs there, playing "This Little Piggy." Provide less support as your baby learns to do this himself. You can also encourage your baby to play with one foot at a time, making sure you bend the knee of the leg remaining on the floor so that he feels his heel touch the floor. Make sure his head stays centered as he plays with each foot, and be sure to repeat the exercise for each leg.

My sitter leaves my baby in her seat for long periods of time. Is this all right?

Babies should spend at least half of their waking time on the floor. By moving on the floor, they practice balance and develop muscle tone. Babies who spend all day sitting in infant seats are robbed of opportunities to build muscle tone and strength, and to move freely. Tell your sitter to limit seat time to brief periods; I recommend a maximum of 20 minutes, 3 times a day.

My baby is only 4 months old and my doctor thinks we should see a therapist. I don't understand why. Does this mean my baby will be slow?

It means you have a good doctor! Often a careful, skilled physician will refer a baby for a neurodevelopmental evaluation. For instance, if a 4-month-old baby is unable to hold his head centered, still has trouble lifting his head while he's on his tummy, or has difficulty reaching forward, a good physician may want to see if early therapy is warranted. Frequently, babies are referred just to be sure that they're developing on target.

(Many of the babies referred to me for evaluation don't need any intervention at all.) And many babies who *do* need intervention are able to catch up with their peers, so don't hesitate to obtain help.

PARENTS' STORIES

ELLIE

Ellie was so demanding! She wanted to be held constant-ly. And when she learned to drop her toys, she expected me to play "fetch" constantly. I loved playing with her, but sometimes I needed a break—even if it was just to take a shower.

We bought Ellie a toy called an exersaucer. Ellie can sit up in it without assistance, and it has toys attached with suction cups so she can grab the toys and release them, without me having to pick them up. Now she's perfectly happy for 15 or 20 minutes at a time, and I can take showers in peace—or sometimes even read a magazine article!

JOHN

John puts everything, and I mean everything, *in his mouth. I know it's normal, but I worried that he'd swallow some-thing dangerous.*

My husband and I created a "safe area" for John, so he could explore objects safely. I spread a clean blanket on the floor, and constructed a barrier around it. I put toys of all different sizes and shapes and textures in this area, being sure to keep them clean—and being sure that none of the toys had small or sharp parts. Now he can gum toys to his heart's content, and I don't have to worry.

KARA

Kara's birth certificate from China said she was 6 months old, but my adopted baby couldn't hold her head up. Her lit-tle ribs poked out, and she didn't even look at me.

Our pediatrician said therapy could help Kara catch up. First the therapist put Kara on her side and placed a rattle about an inch from Kara's hand, teaching her to reach for it. Up on a soft, big ball, Kara learned to move her legs and roll over as the ball rocked her gently. With a large circular pillow called a Bop Cushion, Kara learned to lift her head when she was on her tummy, and later to sit up.

Kara had therapy for about 6 months before she "graduated," able to do all of the things that other babies her age could do. Now she's 3 years old. She stands on tiptoes, wearing her ballet leotard and tiny pink shoes, and she waves at me as I watch her taking part in a "pre-ballet class." Kara's therapy took some time and some effort, but when I see her dance, I know the results were well worth the work!

CHLOE

Chloe's huge blue eyes looked at me. "Uh, uh," she said. Gotta move. She would fuss if left for more than 10 minutes in the infant seat or on the floor. The fussing and grunting drove me bananas. I was tired of being a full-time baby entertainer. Chloe needed changes of scenery and position since she couldn't yet move herself.

After breakfast, I put Chloe in the excersaucer in the bathroom while I took a shower. She liked spinning and hearing the water. While I changed and dressed, I put her on the floor, laying her on her side, using the bop cushion. Sometimes we moved to the baby swing or stroller. Chloe became so much happier. The "Circuit"—sitting, excersaucer, bouncer, swing, bop cushion, Gymfinity—was a great help to me.

Chapter Four

I Can Sit Up

It's amazing. Just a few months ago you were "oohing" and "ahhing" over the cute baby clothes you received at your baby shower—and now you're out shopping for a whole new wardrobe! That's because your baby is growing like a weed. In the first 6 to 8 months of life, your baby will double his weight and grow as much as 6 inches.

In addition to getting bigger and stronger every day, your baby is growing more and more curious about the world. He loves going out for walks in the stroller. He also loves to imitate you, and patty-cake is his favorite game. He'll avidly watch videotapes about other babies. He "coos" all the time—the first step toward talking. He likes to play with other people's hair, and enjoys bath time (especially when he's splashing water everywhere).

Both of your baby's hands are open most of the time now, and he can move his fingers separately. He's beginning to be able to hold toys (mostly he'll grasp them for a second and then drop them), and soon he'll start putting them in his mouth. Any day now he'll start teething, so you'll need a good supply of bibs.

Your baby's mind, like his body, is growing and changing. For instance, he's gaining a better understanding now of "object permanence," the knowledge that people and things still exist even when they're not in sight. A fun way to encourage this understanding is by playing peek-a-boo—but with a few twists. For instance, cover your baby's foot ,then say "peek-a-boo!" and uncover it with a flourish. Or cover your face and then move slightly to your baby's left or right side before revealing yourself. You can even hide your face behind your baby's feet! Also, try hiding toys, pets, and different body parts when you play peek-a-boo.

Here's another way to turn a simple game of peek-a-boo into an educational experience. When you play this game using a toy, start by hiding only *part* of the toy; this will allow your baby to gradually grasp the concept of object permanence. Also, try covering objects with a cloth that has holes your baby can peek through—or use cellophane so your baby can see the toy underneath.

Patty-cake is more than just a game, too. When your baby plays patty-cake, he learns to bring his hands together at the midline of his body, practices coordinating his eyes and hands, and gains a better understanding of spatial concepts including together/apart, in/out, up/down, and on/off.

GRADUATING TO SITTING

Another major skill your baby will begin practicing around this time is sitting up. Imagine how exciting this is for a baby who's been limited to a floor-level view for months! Sitting will open new horizons for your baby, allowing him to see and interact with the world from an entirely new perspective.

Your baby has been preparing for sitting for several months. On his tummy, he's been learning to push up and lift his head against gravity. He's also been learning to use his arms to support some of his weight—a skill he'll need later, to get into and out of sitting, and to catch himself with his arms when he loses his balance.

By "swimming" or pivoting in a circle on his tummy, your baby is learning to shift his weight from side to side, and forward and back. This is a crucial skill, because he'll need to shift his weight to sit successfully. (Otherwise, if he looks to one side or gets jostled, he'll fall over.) And when he rocks forward and backward while keeping his head up and centered, he improves his head control and shoulder stability— also critical elements in sitting.

For all of these reasons, it's important to place your infant on his tummy frequently during play times. However, he may not prefer this position, which takes more effort than being on his back. Start him out with just a few minutes of "tummy play" at a time, and gradually extend his tummy periods as he grows more confident. If your baby fusses when he's on his tummy, provide him with entertainment and praise, and he'll be more willing to make the effort. (Remember, of course, not to let your baby sleep on his tummy! If he falls asleep while playing, immediately move him onto his back.)

If your baby continues to fuss and cry when placed on his tummy, provide him with some support so he's not doing all of the work himself. Have him play while lying on his tummy over your lap, or put a foam wedge or rolled-up towel under his chest, or hold him over the arm of a sofa. This will allow him to practice all of the important tummy-play skills while being safe and secure.

Some parents try to hurry their babies into sitting up, by placing them in a sitting position before the babies are ready. Sitting your baby up too early, however, can be scary for him. If your baby's back is rounded when he sits, or he can't yet push up on his arms and play when he's on his tummy, be patient and provide him with more opportunities to develop his skills through "tummy play." Then, when he *is* ready to sit, he'll be able to do it proudly and successfully.

THE BUILDING BLOCKS OF SITTING

To build a tower of blocks, you have to place each block just right. Otherwise, your tower will tip over. Similarly, your baby will sit correctly only if all of the different components—building blocks—of sitting have developed in the correct sequence.

One of the most important of those components is your baby's tummy muscles. Well-developed tummy muscles provide stability, allow your baby to keep her back straight, and help her right herself when her balance is upset. Your baby's tummy muscles connect the upper and lower parts of her body, so that she's able to balance by shifting her weight from side to side and forward and backward. In addition, your baby will use her tummy muscles to bring her legs together when she sits.

Head control is another important part of sitting up. Your baby's head is about half her body weight, and that's a lot to support! She can't sit safely without help until she can hold her head up in midline, and bring it back to the center if it falls forward, backward, or to the side.

Your baby also needs to learn to sit symmetrically, with

her back straight and her body centered in midline—not sagging to one side, tilted backward, or slouched forward. A straight, well-developed back now may help prevent back problems, neck pain, and pinched nerves later in life.

Your baby's arms play an important role in sitting as well, because she needs to learn to bring her arms forward or to the side quickly if she loses her balance. This skill, called "protective extension," keeps her from falling over and protects her head from injury.

Some babies have difficulty mastering one or more of these skills. The most common blocks to sitting are:

🐣 Baby lacks head control.

🐣 Baby's back bends to one side, or is rounded.

🐣 Baby lacks balance, and is afraid of falling.

🐣 Baby falls because she can't put her arms out to catch herself.

The exercises in this chapter address all of these problem areas, and work on each building block of successful sitting. Be sure to begin with the first two pre-sitting exercises. Some babies will be able to do these exercises easily, while others need a little extra practice.

BABY'S SKILLS TO START

Before beginning the exercises in this chapter, be sure your baby has these skills:

- 🎲 I can hold my head up and keep it centered, and reach for a toy without moving my head
- 🎲 I can put my hands together
- 🎲 I can roll from my side to my tummy, and bring my arms forward
- 🎲 While on my tummy, I can lift my head up straight, push up on my extended arms, and go around in a circle, clockwise and counterclockwise
- 🎲 On my back, I can lift my legs and touch my knees or toes

If your baby is still mastering these skills, the exercises in the previous chapter will prepare him so that he'll be successful in learning to sit independently.

EXERCISES

Parent As a Playground

SKILLS TO BUILD

- Becoming more comfortable on tummy
- Holding head up while pushing up with forearms
- Developing the back extension necessary to sit independently
- Developing shoulder stability
- Using arms to protect against falling

EQUIPMENT

- Any toy that makes a sound or moves

EXERCISE

- Sit on a couch or on the floor. Place your baby tummy down, draped over your lap. Make sure that his arms are forward, and that he's supporting his weight on his forearms. Position him so that his body is in a straight line, with his legs close together.  Keep your legs close together, so he doesn't fall between your legs.
- Encourage your baby to look at the toy and play with it in this position for 3 to 5 minutes.
- As your baby gets better at keeping his head up and his back straight, gradually decrease angle.

Parent As a Chair

SKILLS TO BUILD
- Increased strength in tummy muscles
- Sitting with a straight back
- Shifting weight from side to side
- Using arms to protect against falling

EXERCISE
- Sit on a well padded floor and hold your baby firmly against your body, facing forward, between your legs. Her back should be straight and well supported by your tummy and  chest. Provide additional support by holding your legs firmly against your baby's sides, if necessary. Make sure your baby's legs are fairly straight and her feet are pointing up. (If your baby slumps, gently push her shoulders back toward your body. If she continues to slouch, raise her arms gently.)
- As your baby becomes comfortable with this sitting position, gently shift your weight to one side by rocking sideways (this shifts your baby to one side).
- Provide support as necessary so your baby catches herself by putting her arms on your leg and comes back to a sitting position.

NOTE: If your baby's bottom slips forward or she has difficulty bending at the hips, do *not* do this exercise without consulting your doctor.

Hug the Ball

SKILLS TO BUILD
- Using arms to protect against falling
- Shifting weight forward and backward
- Practicing sitting up straight and tall

EQUIPMENT
- Soft inflatable or cloth ball, 12–18 inches in diameter

EXERCISE
- Sit on a well padded floor, or on a bed or sofa, and place your baby in front of you, sitting up and facing forward, with his back well supported and his knees not more than 4 inches apart.
- Provide support at his knees and legs, to keep his legs fairly straight (knees not turned way out) and his arms forward. Be sure his back is straight. Place a soft ball, 12–18 inches in diameter, in front of him.
- Encourage your baby to keep his arms forward, hold on to the ball, and practice pushing against the ball for balance.
- Try this exercise with different sizes of balls.

NOTE: If your baby's legs are widely turned out, support his knees and gently turn them in so his feet are straight.

NOTE: Playing with a larger ball will provide more support to keep your baby upright. As he grows more skillful at balancing, use a smaller ball.

Tummy Toner

SKILLS TO BUILD

- Tucking chin to chest and keeping head forward when tilted, to keep from falling backward
- Keeping arms forward and head in midline when tilted backward

EXERCISE

- Place your baby on your lap, facing to your left. Make sure she keeps her head forward and in midline, with her arms forward.
- Support your baby with both hands—one at her back and the other on her tummy—to give her the feeling of how her tummy and back muscles work together. Be sure she's not slumped.

- Lift your left leg and tilt your baby backward VERY slowly, about 1 inch. Keep your arms around your baby's body, and be sure her arms are forward.
- Gradually increase how much you tilt your leg, as your baby is able to counterbalance. You'll notice her knees bending up, her tummy firming and her chin tucking down.
- Turn your baby to the other side and repeat.

NOTE: If your baby's legs are widely spread, bring them closer together. If her legs stiffen or she continually falls backward, choose another exercise and consult your physician. Make sure you provide gentle support to baby's tummy, without pushing.

Take a Trip

SKILLS TO BUILD

- Practicing getting arms forward
- Learning to take weight over arms, and developing arm strength and shoulder stability
- Developing skills to prevent head injury

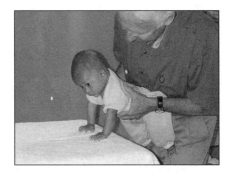

EQUIPMENT

- Make sure baby is wearing soft clothes or cotton "onesie"

EXERCISE

- Hold your baby securely under his arms with both sides of his chest well supported.
- Walk around the house and gently bring your baby down so he can get both arms forward and practice taking weight over his arms on a sofa or well padded floor.
- Gently and slowly rock your baby back and forth with his arms on a surface for 10–30 seconds.
- You can also practice having your baby push a door closed with his hands while holding him in a more vertical position.
- Be very alert to prevent your baby from nose-diving and/or bumping his head.

On the following page is a progress chart you can use to follow your baby's motor skills. If your baby is a preemie or developmentally delayed, some or all of these skills will appear later than they are shown on the chart.

BABY MOTOR SKILLS

MONTH	3.5	4	4.5	5	6	7	8	9
Brings one or both arms to middle of body while lying on his back; reaches for a toy while on back	👣	👣	👣	👣	👣	👣	👣	👣
Holds a toy for 10–30 seconds			👣	👣	👣	👣	👣	👣
Can sit with a fairly straight back, head in the middle, when supported			👣	👣	👣	👣	👣	👣
Can come back to center when off balance (5–45 degrees)			👣	👣	👣	👣	👣	👣
Uses feet to push against the floor when lying on side, tummy, or back			👣	👣	👣	👣	👣	👣
Can push up and play with both arms forward, while lying on tummy			👣	👣	👣	👣	👣	👣
Rolls from tummy to back and from back to tummy				👣	👣	👣	👣	👣
Can lift legs off floor and play with toes while lying on back				👣	👣	👣	👣	👣
Using arms, will catch herself to maintain sitting position				👣	👣	👣	👣	👣
Plays with feet and rolls from side to side while lying on back				👣	👣	👣	👣	👣

IMPORTANT: Every baby develops differently. These skills can emerge as late as the last time listed on the chart, and still be well within normal limits.

I CAN DRINK FROM A CUP
AND EAT WITH A SPOON

When your baby is able to sit, she's ready to learn to use a cup and a spoon at mealtime. Parents often have mixed feelings about taking this step, because a baby with a cup or spoon is a huge mess waiting to happen. However, the benefits to your baby will far outweigh the extra cleanups and laundry that her experiments will generate. Drinking from a cup and eating from a spoon will help your baby develop the oral motor skills that she'll need, a few months from now, in order to speak clearly and easily. Among the skills she'll learn:

- When she uses her lips to take food off her spoon, she'll practice closing her lips—an act that's necessary to produce "m," "b," and "p" sounds. (Keeping her lips closed also prepares her to keep her mouth closed when she chews food later on.)
- As she drinks from a cup, she'll refine the movements of her lips and tongue in preparation for saying words.
- When she moves food from a spoon into her mouth, she'll be moving her tongue behind her teeth—a skill required to make "s" and "d" sounds, and sound blends.
- Swallowing solid and textured foods will teach her to chew with her mouth closed, develop her jaw strength and stability, and help to prevent drooling.

In short, cups and spoons aren't just eating utensils for your baby; they're educational tools as well. So break out the bibs, and prepare to make a mess—and remember that it's for a good cause!

EXERCISES

Lip Smack

SKILLS TO BUILD
- Keeping lips closed
- Bringing upper lip down and putting both lips together, in preparation for early speech
- Jaw stability and improved oral motor tone, which help your baby to say sounds that require lip closure, such as "m," "p," "b"

EXERCISE
- Place your baby on your lap in a sitting position or in an infant seat. Make sure her back is straight, and her head is aligned with her body, and well forward.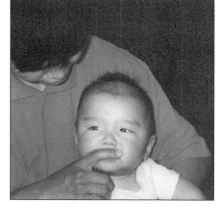
- Use your index finger to gently bring your baby's top lip down so that her lips are together. Provide support to her lower jaw and lip as needed to keep her mouth closed.
- Smack your lips together and encourage your baby to imitate you. Give her time to respond, and cue her, if necessary, by stroking her top lip.

Spoon-Feeding

SKILLS TO BUILD

- Improved tongue, lip, and mouth coordination, in preparation for early speech
- Using upper lip to take food off the spoon
- Using lips together to say "m," "b," and "p" sounds.

EQUIPMENT

- Small baby spoon

EXERCISE

- Use a small baby spoon, not a regular teaspoon. A smaller spoon allows your baby to close his lips completely around the spoon.
- Place a well-filled spoon on your baby's lower lip.
- Wait for your baby to use his upper lip to take food off the spoon (rather than scraping food off the spoon onto the roof of his mouth).

NOTE: Always keep your baby's head well forward when he's eating, to prevent choking. Feed him in an infant seat or high chair.

NOTE: While feeding solid foods, make sure your baby closes his mouth after every bite. If necessary, use your index finger to bring his top lip down. You can use an additional finger to support his lower jaw so that he can close his mouth.

Cup Drinking

SKILLS TO BUILD

- Using lips to feed and swallow
- Controlling the flow of liquid by using upper lip
- Closing lips
- Swallowing and breathing with mouth closed

EQUIPMENT

- Small, flexible plastic cup with a thickened drink (ideally formula or breast milk mixed with cereal; it should be the consistency of buttermilk)

EXERCISE

- Place your baby in a sitting position on your lap, or in an infant seat or high chair. Make sure her head is centered, *straight up,* and well forward. With one hand, stabilize her head and keep it forward.
- With your other hand, place the cup on your baby's lower lip and slowly let a *small* amount of liquid (½ tsp.) flow into her mouth.
- Remove the cup and encourage your baby to close her lips. Gently push her top lip down if necessary. Encourage her to swallow with her lips closed.
- Repeat the exercise.

NOTE: Do *not* do this if your baby chokes or has *any* sort of congestion.

NOTE: If your baby is tube-fed, consult your pediatrician before doing *any* oral feeding.

Baby Toothbrush

If you don't want to spend the next four or five years struggling with your child over toothbrushing, it's a smart idea to get him accustomed to tooth and gum care now!

SKILLS TO BUILD
- Exploring texture and input in mouth, in preparation for eating solid food
- Desensitization to gums and mouth being touched, in preparation for toothbrushing and good dental care throughout life

EQUIPMENT
- For Exercise I: no equipment needed
- For Exercise II: baby finger toothbrush—slips over parent's finger, available at drugstore

EXERCISE I: GUMMY TOOTHBRUSH

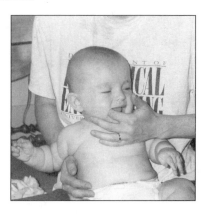

- Place your baby in an infant seat, with his head in midline.
- Gently press on your baby's outer gum line, using your finger.
- Begin at the center of your baby's bottom gum and slowly move your finger along the right edge of his gum line. Encourage your baby to close his jaws and swallow.
- Do this exercise to both the right and left side of your baby's mouth. Do each side separately, **without crossing the center of your baby's mouth.**
- Repeat, alternating top and bottom gums.

EXERCISE II: BABY TOOTHBRUSH
- Place the finger toothbrush on your index finger. Make sure the brush is tightly on your finger (to prevent it from falling off and choking your baby). Carefully and slowly massage your baby's gums from middle to side.
- Do this three times on each side, encouraging your baby to close his mouth as you "brush." Make sure your baby's head stays in midline.

NOTE: Be sure that your baby's head and neck are forward to prevent choking and gagging.

NOTE: If your baby does not like this exercise, try using your finger alone—or use a warm terry cloth washcloth.

Here is a progress chart you can use to follow your baby's feeding skills. If your baby is a preemie or developmentally delayed, some or all of these skills will appear later than they are shown on the chart.

BABY'S FEEDING SKILLS

MONTH	2.5	3	3.5	4	4.5	5	5.5	6	6.5	7
Anticipates feeding	🍼	🍼	🍼	🍼	🍼	🍼	🍼	🍼	🍼	🍼
Smacks lips		🍼	🍼	🍼	🍼	🍼	🍼	🍼	🍼	🍼
Sucks cheeks to make an "O"			🍼	🍼	🍼	🍼	🍼	🍼	🍼	🍼
Takes food from a spoon, using upper lip				🍼	🍼	🍼	🍼	🍼	🍼	🍼
Sticks out tongue in imitation					🍼	🍼	🍼	🍼	🍼	🍼
Clicks tongue						🍼	🍼	🍼	🍼	🍼
Drinks from Tipee cup (spout) with help						🍼	🍼	🍼	🍼	🍼

IMPORTANT: Every baby develops differently. These skills can emerge as late as the last time listed on the chart, and still be well within normal limits.

LEARNING AND PLAYING

If you're thinking of buying a baby walker or baby bouncer, save your money. Why? Because these two popular baby items can do far more harm than good.

Baby walkers and bouncers can cause babies to stiffen their legs, and can prevent them from developing the head, arm, and tummy control they'll need to sit and walk correctly. In addition to interfering with normal development, walkers and bouncers can be unsafe, and occasionally cause spinal fractures, hip dislocations, and head injuries. A far better alternative to walkers or bouncers is an exersaucer. However, if your baby seems stiff, falls to one side, or can't hold his head up, don't use an exersaucer.

You don't really need *any* special equipment, because simply moving around on the floor is the best exercise for all babies. During floor play, your baby can explore spatial concepts such as in/out, up/down, depth perception, and position in space, without worrying about falling.

Good toys for babies at this age include ones that can be manipulated—for instance, large, soft sponges and blocks that can be grasped, squeezed, and stacked. Musical toys, such as bells and maracas, are great fun and can help develop listening skills. Here's an easy game: hide a bell under a blanket, shake the bell, and ask your baby, "Where's bell?" Wait for him to look, and then shake the bell again. This game teaches "auditory localization"—a fancy term for the ability to figure out the location of a sound.

Select light, fairly small toys (generally not larger than 3 to 4 inches in diameter) that fit easily into your baby's hand. Spinning toys, a favorite at this stage, will improve your baby's manual dexterity and help increase his attention span. Encourage your baby to play with a toy for up to 5 minutes, and give him about 3 books and toys to play with each day. At this age, he doesn't need a confusing array of fancy toys; he's better off with a few basics that he can explore thoroughly.

Be sure to read to your baby every day, even if it's just for a few minutes. Reading time is relaxing for both of you, and you can use books to teach your baby important concepts. For instance, you can demonstrate "object permanence" by covering up pictures in his books and then revealing them. Books with push buttons that make music or animal noises will help your baby understand cause and effect—in other words, he'll learn that "I can make things happen!" And reading can help him learn to "eye point"—that is, to direct his gaze toward specific objects pictured in books.

At this age, your baby enjoys interacting with you as you read. He can help turn the pages, and you and he can take turns patting pictures or pushing the buttons on push-button books. By now, your baby can pay attention to a book for 5 to 10 minutes, and will actually start to remember his favorite parts of books and look forward to seeing them.

BEST BOOKS FOR THIS AGE:

- Books with realistic photos and objects
- Books with parts baby can move (e.g., plastic bunny fits in slots of book, door opens)
- Simple push-button books with one or two buttons that play songs or animal sounds
- Books with either an animal or toy attached by a ribbon
- Books with squeakers or toys attached
- Pop-up books
- Books with embedded objects
- Small book (3 inches) that can be held easily
- Books about familiar objects and babies—baby in car seat, baby with bottle, baby in bath
- Books that feature Mom or Dad and baby together

Toy/Equipment	Skill

Exersaucer

1. Allows your child to sit and move independently, promoting autonomy and self-confidence
2. Allows your child to explore her position in space, spin, bend, and straighten legs
3. Teaches balance and eye/hand coordination
4. Teaches separation of movement between upper and lower extremities

Pop-Up Jack-in-the-Box

1. Teaches follow-through; attention span; repetition
2. Teaches delayed gratification
3. Improves manual dexterity and hand function
4. Teaches concept of spatial orientation: in/out, through, beside, between, up/down
5. Improves motor planning skills

Touch Me Book

1. Stimulates sense of touch
2. Builds auditory memory skills and teaches your baby to follow directions ("Pat the Bunny")
3. Increases your child's vocabulary and understanding of language
4. Improves fine motor coordination

I Can Sit Up

Large, Patterned Sponge Blocks

1. Improves fine motor coordination
2. Helps your baby explore spatial concepts: height, depth, spatial relationship/stacking
3. Improves your baby's ability to grasp and release
4. Teaches visual discrimination: size and shape

Couvallis

1. Improves visual tracking and focus skills
2. Develops grasp and release skills, thumb and opposition
3. Improves auditory awareness/listening skills
4. Teaches your baby to anticipate an event

Suction Cup Toy

1. Allows your child to play independently
2. Teaches cause-and-effect: when your child pushes the toy, it makes a sound and moves
3. Improves eye/hand coordination
4. Teaches your baby to reach across the midline of his body
5. Teaches your baby to move his arm and head independently

BABY STEPS

Baby Bop Cushion

1. Allows your baby to explore sitting position with safety
2. Encourages your baby to push up when placed down on tummy

Smart Stick

1. Teaches baby to point
2. Develops independent finger movement
3. Teaches cause/effect—push button produces sound
4. Teaches sounds/animals

Baby in a Basket

SKILLS TO BUILD

- Sitting independently and safely
- Balancing and shifting weight from side to side, with support
- Playing independently in a sitting position

EQUIPMENT

- A flexible plastic *vented* laundry basket
- Soft toys and a thin blanket (if needed)
- Velcro links to attach toys to basket

EXERCISE

- Place your baby in the laundry basket and let her become comfortable playing in a sitting position. (Line basket with a cotton blanket.)
- Very slowly and gently lift the laundry basket 2–3 inches, so that it tilts to one side, and say, "Tilt!" Your baby should shift her weight to the opposite side, to keep from falling over.
- Explore tilting forward and backward in small increments.
- If your baby is fearful or stiff, try this exercise with the basket on your lap.

NOTE: Don't leave your baby unattended in the basket! Make sure your baby doesn't get her fingers stuck in vents of the basket. String or attach toys to the basket or place a few soft toys in the basket.

BABY STEPS

Here is a progress chart you can use to follow your baby's learning skills. If your baby is a preemie or developmentally delayed, some or all of these skills will appear later than they are shown on the chart.

BABY'S LEARNING SKILLS

Month	5	5.5	6	6.5	7	8	9
Uses two hands together	👣	👣	👣	👣	👣	👣	👣
Holds toy with one hand and uses other hand to squeak toy	👣	👣	👣	👣	👣	👣	👣
Puts objects in mouth	👣	👣	👣	👣	👣	👣	
Points to objects	👣	👣	👣	👣	👣	👣	👣
Shakes rattle or bells	👣	👣	👣	👣	👣	👣	👣
Transfers objects from hand to hand	👣	👣	👣	👣	👣	👣	👣
Bats at hanging objects 5–10 times	👣	👣	👣	👣	👣	👣	👣
Imitates lip-smacking, patting, sticking tongue out when demonstrated by adult	👣	👣	👣	👣	👣	👣	👣
Touches pages in a book	👣	👣	👣	👣	👣	👣	👣
Responds to large objects in picture books by looking (eye pointing)	👣	👣	👣	👣	👣	👣	👣
Rolls or pushes ball	👣	👣	👣	👣	👣	👣	👣
Enjoys knocking down soft blocks or stacked cups	👣	👣	👣	👣	👣	👣	👣
Tries to turn pages in a book		👣	👣	👣	👣	👣	👣

IMPORTANT: Every baby develops differently. These skills can emerge as late as the last time listed on the chart, and still be well within normal limits.

I Can Sit Up

BABY'S ACCOMPLISHMENTS

After the exercises in this chapter have been completed successfully, your baby will have the following skills:

🖐 I can sit with my head centered, my arms forward, my legs and back fairly straight, and my feet pointed up

🖐 I can reach easily to either side and cross the midline of my body to grasp an object

🖐 I can quickly and consistently reach my arms out to the front and sideways to protect my head, if I fall forward or to the side

🖐 When I'm off balance, I can right myself without falling, by shifting my weight sideways, forward or slightly backward

"CAN YOU TELL ME WHY...?"
Answers to Questions Parents Often Ask

Will putting my baby in a walker at this age help him to walk earlier?

No! A walker or Johnny Jump Up will not help your baby's hip sockets to develop—a prerequisite for walking. That's because most of your baby's weight is borne by the seat of the equipment. Also, in a walker or jumper, your baby may sit with his body out of alignment, his spine, back, or feet curved unnaturally. Being on the floor to play freely is best.

My baby doesn't like being on her tummy on the floor. Can't we just skip the tummy position?

Exercising on the floor in the tummy position helps your baby learn to shift her weight safely, and helps her neck, back, hip, and leg muscles work together so she can lift against gravity. All of these skills are important for crawling and walking. So don't stop putting your baby on her tummy; instead, make this position more fun for her. Try putting a moving musical toy in front of her on the floor, to keep her entertained while she's on her tummy, or put her over your lap or on your tummy and read a story.

My baby won't sit with her legs straight. Is this a problem?

Your baby is probably sitting in either a "ring" position or a "W" position. Almost all babies sit in these two positions occasionally. Babies who *always* sit in either the "W" or the ring position, however, need help to learn other ways of sitting. Otherwise, they may be delayed in learning to crawl and walk. The key word, again, is **always**. If your baby **only** sits in one of these positions, check with your physician. (Also check with your doctor if your baby is very stiff at this age, or constantly keeps her toes pointed.)

You can help your baby learn to sit with her legs in front and closer together by sitting behind her and holding her legs together while you play with her.

My baby sticks her big toes up when I touch her feet. Is this normal?

For the first few months some babies will lift their big toes up high, separate from the rest of their toes. This is called a Babinski reflex. This foot reflex should be gone by 4 months of age, but it's perfectly normal before then.

Some children have very sensitive feet, and will stiffen or curl their toes in response to pressure on their feet. If your baby does this, avoid pushing against her feet. When she stands with support, encourage her to stand with her feet flat on the floor.

My baby only sits on the sofa, or when he's propped up by pillows or placed on a Bop Cushion. He can't sit alone. What should I do?

Your baby needs to practice "protective extension"— catching himself with his arms if he starts to fall. You can help him learn this skill by practicing the "Parent as a Chair" and "Take a Trip" exercises in this chapter.

I want to buy my baby a high chair. How old does she need to be in order to sit safely in a high chair?

Actually, it's not a matter of age. Your baby will be ready for a high chair when her back is strong enough that she can sit up straight. Try this test: when your baby is on her tummy on the floor, can she push up on her extended arms? If so, it's high chair time.

My baby keeps trying to sit forward in his infant seat and car seat. He doesn't seem comfortable. He used to love his infant seat, but now he whines when I put him in it. Is something wrong?

No! Your baby is trying to tell you that he's ready to sit up straighter. He's learning to pull up against gravity, and now he wants to be upright—so adjust his infant seat so that it's not tilted back as far. Also, many babies—especially boys—would rather be on the move than sitting still. If your baby is the active type, let him spend more time on the floor, or in an exersaucer.

I Can Sit Up

PARENTS' STORIES

ERIC

We were so proud when Eric learned to sit up, but we worried because he couldn't do it right. *Instead of sitting up straight, he'd slump forward. Then he'd slowly "jackknife," with his back falling forward or sideways. We had to prop him up with soft pillows, and keep hard plastic toys away from him so he wouldn't fall over on them.*

At Eric's 6-month checkup, his pediatrician gave us some simple exercises to do. Eric and his Daddy did the "Parent as a Chair" and "Parent as a Playground" exercises. Also, I'd lay Eric on his tummy over my lap so he could "seesaw," using his tummy and hip muscles together with his back and shoulders. The exercises worked: soon Eric was sitting up straight, and even playing "roll the ball" with us.

MORGAN

"Timber!" That's what we said all day long. Every time Morgan tried to sit, she'd fall over. She could sit for a few seconds, but then, Boom! She couldn't reach even 2 or 3 inches for a toy without tipping over.

Fortunately, the nurse at our baby class had scheduled a pediatric therapist to speak about infant development. The therapist helped us understand that in order to sit, babies must develop "graded" balance—that is, they must learn to compensate when nudged or jostled, rather than toppling over. This type of balance develops in millimeters. She also explained that Morgan needed to practice using her arms to catch herself and support her weight if she fell.

To help Morgan develop faster reactions, we practiced putting her arms down (slowly and gently at first) while we supported her arms at her shoulders. We also worked on exercises that improved her balance. Now she can sit up well, and catch herself if she falls. The other day our golden retriever gave her a big wet kiss, and she managed to stay upright. We were impressed!

I Can Crawl

A revolutionary event is about to occur in your baby's life. Up to now, he's been at your mercy. If you set him down in the kitchen, he was stuck in the kitchen. If you plopped him in a boring spot in the living room, he couldn't budge.

Now, he's about to get his revenge.

In a few weeks, your baby will learn to crawl, and your life will never be the same. He's going to be going everywhere and getting into everything. If you turn your back on him for a few seconds he'll be in another room, or maybe even another time zone.

To protect your little explorer, you'll need to fully childproof your house, if you haven't already done so. Be sure the cords of blinds and curtains are out of reach. Put safety plugs in electrical outlets, and locks on cabinet doors. Remove any toxic substances—cleansers, bug sprays, makeup—from low cabinets, and make sure plants are out of reach. Also be careful when you're eating or drinking around your baby, because at this age your baby will grab for cups or plates. I can't tell you how many horror stories I've heard involving cups of hot coffee left within reach of overly curious infants. (Be careful when you're carrying your baby, too, because at this stage, he'll grab a cup or plate right out of your hand.)

Remember that your baby's goal at this stage is simple: Move, move, move! Even if he's not crawling yet, he's no longer content to sit or lie placidly on the floor, watching the world go by. He needs frequent changes in position and scenery. One way to satisfy him safely, and maintain your sanity, is to create a baby exercise circuit. Set up a baby swing, an exersaucer, and a toy area, and rotate him through these activities. He'll be developing his muscles and learning about depth perception and spatial relationships (in/out, up/down, low/high), and you'll have at least a little peace and quiet.

While your baby is perfecting his motor skills, you'll want to perfect a different skill: ducking. That's because your baby is exploring movement in space, and cause/effect relationships, using the simple scientific technique of throwing every toy or household object he can get his hands on. It's a challenging stage for you, but very educational for him! Believe it or not, the skills he's learning now may stand him in good stead someday if he becomes an architect, engineer, designer, or inventor.

TIME TO CRAWL!

Your baby probably is anxious to crawl—and that's good, because crawling is a major milestone in his physical and intellectual development. Crawling teaches the left and right sides of your baby's brain to work together, enhancing his thinking skills and integrating his senses.

Crawling also develops strength and fine motor coordination in your baby's wrists and fingers, preparing him for such later skills as dressing, zipping, buttoning, coloring, writing, toothbrushing, and holding a knife and fork. In addition, crawling strengthens his shoulders, arms, and upper body, and helps refine his "protective extension"—the reaction in which his arms come out to catch him if he falls, protecting his head from injury.

Crawling improves your baby's balance and coordination, and it helps him learn to use his legs together, teaching him good motor patterns for walking. Crawling is especially important for babies who are stronger on one side than the other, because it teaches them to use both sides of their body equally. For babies with low muscle tone, crawling helps to develop strength and stability in the shoulders and hips.

Most babies are anxious to crawl, but some—for instance, large babies—may need lots of practice. In fact, some children never learn to crawl on their own, but instead scoot on their bottoms, or roll, or inch forward on their backs. If your baby isn't crawling by the time he's 9 or 10 months old, a therapist can provide exercises to help him catch up. That's important, because a baby who skips crawling may suffer later as a result. (Many children who have trouble in kindergarten, for instance, either crawled late or skipped the crawling stage entirely.)

The exercises in this chapter focus on many of the skills needed for successful crawling. In particular, several exercises work on body rotation, an important component of learning to crawl. When your baby rotates, he crosses midline, reaching from one side of his body to the opposite side. This activity makes both sides of the brain work together, building new brain pathways that will enhance sensory motor and cognitive skills.

SKILLS THAT CRAWLING BUILDS

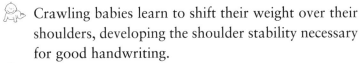 Crawling babies learn to shift their weight over their shoulders, developing the shoulder stability necessary for good handwriting.

Crawling integrates the two sides of the brain. This integration is necessary for a wide range of mental skills, including distinguishing letters, reading, and spelling.

Crawling teaches your baby to bend one side of his body while straightening the other. This improves the skills he needs for physical play and sports.

Crawling helps your baby integrate input from several of his senses at once—a skill that's necessary for all learning.

Crawling integrates your baby's sensory system (which provides input to the brain from the senses) and his motor system (which stimulates movement).

Crawling teaches your baby to hold his legs together and stabilizes his hips, which will give him a stable "base" when he walks.

Is Your Baby Ready to Crawl?

When your baby can sit with her back straight, roll, shift her weight from side to side when sitting, bring her arms forward, and push up on her tummy, using her tummy muscles, she has the prerequisite skills to crawl. *Make sure she has these skills before you work on crawling.* Crawling *early* isn't important, but crawling *correctly* is crucial.

It's important not to bypass the crawling stage—so encourage your child to crawl even if she's already pulling up to a standing position.

I Can Crawl

BABY'S SKILLS TO START

Before beginning the exercises in this chapter, be sure your baby has these skills:

- ▣ My neck and back are strong, I can hold my head up well, and I like to push away from you with my hands while being held
- ▣ I can roll with my chin tucked, bending one knee up and bringing my arms forward instead of rolling like a log
- ▣ While I'm on my back, I can bend my knees up and touch my knees/feet to the right or left side
- ▣ My balance is improving. When my balance is upset, my arm will come forward or out to the side, to protect my head from injury and keep me from falling over
- ▣ On my tummy, I can play while supporting my weight on my arms. In this position, I can reach forward or to the side, and knock over a toy or help turn pages in a book
- ▣ When placed in a standing position against a low table or other support, I can take my weight on my feet
- ▣ I can sit independently, with my back fairly straight
- ▣ I can reach to the side to get a toy when I'm sitting, and can play in a sitting position

EXERCISES

Airplane

SKILLS TO BUILD
- Keeping head up and in midline in a crawling position
- Bringing arms forward to support weight over straight arms
- Increasing strength in arms, shoulders, and upper back

EXERCISE

- Standing over your baby, holding him with your hands under his chest, place him in a crawling position on the floor or bed. Use your thumbs, if necessary, to help keep his elbows supported.
- Bring your baby's hands down against the floor or bed, while helping him bring his arms forward so his weight is on them. Keep his shoulders and bottom level with each other, so his body is in a straight line.
- Slowly rock your baby forward, so he gets the feeling of supporting his weight over his straight arms.
- Provide less support as your baby is able to take over. Also, gradually make your movements less predictable by bringing him down more quickly, and tilting him slightly to one side or the other.

TIP: Hold your baby firmly at all times during this exercise. A "nose-dive" is frightening, and could cause an injury.

NOTE: Initially, your baby can practice this exercise on a soft surface such as a sofa or bed. As he learns to bring his arms forward and down when his balance shifts, other surfaces may be used, such as a well-padded floor.

Ride-a-Horsey

SKILLS TO BUILD

- Skill and confidence in supported hands-and-knees position
- Supporting weight on straight arms
- Keeping legs together in preparation for crawling and standing

EXERCISE I

- Lie on your back on the floor, with your knees bent and feet firmly on the floor. Place your baby in a crawling position with her arms on your chest. Her knees and hips  should be bent and held together by your legs. Provide support at your baby's arms and trunk as needed, to keep her arms straight and her chest up.
- As your baby becomes more comfortable, provide less support. Encourage her to stay up on her hands and knees independently.

EXERCISE II

- In the same position, rock slowly backward and forward, and side to side, providing support, if necessary, so that your baby maintains her hands-and-knees position.

- Once your baby is able to maintain the hands-and-knees position and rock forward and sideways with little support, support one of her arms and lift the other arm up so that your baby practices shifting her weight from one side of her body to the other. The goal is for your baby to  maintain her hands-and-knees position while she plays with one arm up.

- Alternate sides.

Baby Roll Up

Your baby has an opportunity to use and develop both sides of his body when he practices moving from sitting to lying on his tummy. This exercise is especially useful if your baby prefers one side, or has trouble sitting with his legs straight and his feet in front.

SKILLS TO BUILD

- Rotating upper body and taking weight on arms while reaching across midline and playing in a side-sitting position
- Confidence in sitting with weight to one side

- Sitting with knees and legs together
- Independence in moving into and out of sitting

EXERCISE I

- With your baby in a sitting position, bend his knees so they are close together. Bring your baby's arms to one side, making sure they are straight, so his trunk is turned to the side and supported by his arms.
- While sitting behind your baby, provide support, if needed, to prevent him from falling forward. Play with him in the side-sitting position.

EXERCISE II

- From the side-sitting position, encourage your baby to shift his weight sideways and move down onto the floor.
- From the floor, encourage your baby to come up into a side-sitting position and then into sitting position.

Towel Crawl

SKILLS TO BUILD

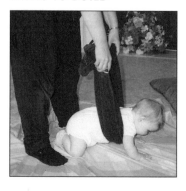

- Gaining skill and confidence in crawling position and learning crawling pattern
- Supporting some weight over arms and legs
- Using both sides of body and brain (helps develop neural pathways important for later learning)

EQUIPMENT

- Small, folded bath towel

EXERCISE

- Place your baby on the floor on his tummy. Wrap the folded towel around his chest, directly below his shoulders, and gently lift him up to a hands-and-knees position. Placing your feet on either side of your baby, use them to keep his knees together. **Make sure the towel is not around your baby's tummy.**
- Allow your baby to become comfortable in the hands-and-knees position, and to take his weight over his extended arms while holding his head up and centered.
- Gently rock your baby forward and backward, pausing in each position so that he becomes comfortable with shifting his weight.
- Gradually pull one side of the towel forward while pulling the other side backward, so your baby experiences a crawling motion.

NOTE: Do this exercise only on a well-padded floor. Be careful to prevent your baby from falling forward in a nosedive.

Here is a progress chart you can use to follow your baby's motor skills. If your baby is a preemie or developmentally delayed, some or all of these skills will appear later than they are shown on the chart.

BABY'S MOTOR SKILLS

Month	5	5.5	6	6.5	7	8	9	10
Supports weight on her hands when on tummy in a crawling position	👣	👣	👣	👣	👣	👣	👣	
On tummy, pushes up using straight arms	👣	👣	👣	👣	👣	👣	👣	
Can move from sitting to side-sitting position	👣	👣	👣	👣	👣	👣	👣	
Moves from sitting position into side-sitting position		👣	👣	👣	👣	👣	👣	
On tummy, gets into crawling position			👣	👣	👣	👣	👣	
Consistently catches himself with straight arms when his balance is upset			👣	👣	👣	👣	👣	
Back is straight when lying over parent's lap on tummy, and legs are together (no curvature in back)				👣	👣	👣	👣	
Plays in side-sitting position							👣	👣
Can roll up into side-sitting position from tummy			👣	👣	👣	👣	👣	👣
Comes up into sitting position from lying on back by rolling to her side and pushing up, using her arms							👣	👣

IMPORTANT: Every baby develops differently. These skills can emerge as late as the last time listed on the chart, and still be well within normal limits.

LEARNING AND PLAYING

A "pre-crawler" or crawling baby can play for up to 5 minutes at a time, and during those play periods she's working hard on the skills that will make her a good student years from now. When she pushes the buttons on a musical toy, she's developing her fine motor coordination. When she listens to stories in picture books, she's improving her attention skills. And when she plays with toys that have parts she can spin, her eyes and hands are learning to work together.

In addition to playing for longer periods, your baby is playing more *actively*. At this age, she's enjoying becoming the master of her little universe. Until now, things have happened to her, but now she's making things happen herself. Buy her toys with wheels to turn, or characters that pop up when she pushes a button. (And give her a free lesson in cause-and-effect by pouring a bit of water on her high chair tray so she can splash.)

Your baby is already starting to understand that there's a big world outside her house, so read her stories about going to the doctor or the grocery store. She'll also enjoy books with repetitive sequences, such as *Good Night Moon*, and books with very simple nursery rhymes or finger games. She's even beginning to understand emotions, so introduce the concepts of "happy" and "sad," showing her different people's faces and expressions in her books.

Your baby is learning 5 to 10 words a day, and you can increase her vocabulary with picture books showing common items (for instance, *My House*). Also, work on teaching her to discriminate different sounds by imitating two different noises—for instance, a cow "mooing" and a dog barking—as you read to her. Encourage her to imitate the beginning sounds of words, and to point to pictures. Big, sturdy books are best at this age, especially if they wipe clean easily. Your baby will enjoy books she can actively manipulate—for instance, those with finger puppets to touch and flaps to open. Push-button books that play music or make sounds are fun, too.

BEST BOOKS FOR THIS AGE:

- Repetitive sequence—*Good Night Moon*
- Books of finger games
- Nursery rhymes—*Three Little Kittens*
- 18-by-24-inch cardboard flap books
- Books with large picture vocabulary—3 to 4 items per page (chair, sofa, mirror, etc.)
- My first words, my house, my family
- Books with elastic and attached animals
- Farm books
- Animal books

Toy/Equipment	**Skill**

Fisher-Price™ Lights Piano

1. Teaches cause-and-effect
2. Promotes manual dexterity
3. Lengthens attention span
4. Improves eye/hand coordination
5. Teaches baby to anticipate an action, improving memory skills
6. Encourages pushing down with open hands
7. Teaches concept of on/off

**Peek-a-Boo™
Lift and Look™ books**

1. Teaches baby to follow directions
2. Increases attention span
3. Improves manual dexterity
4. Teaches turn-taking: parent, then child, turns pages
5. Teaches spatial concepts: up/down, in/out
6. Increases vocabulary and receptive language skills

**Push-Button Phone or
Remote Control Device**

1. Improves fine motor coordination, isolated finger movements, and manual dexterity
2. Teaches cause-and-effect
3. Helps baby learn language concepts
4. Encourages independent play

I Can Crawl

Color Spin

1. Helps baby understand movement in space
2. Teaches concepts of fast/slow, stop/go
3. Improves eye/hand coordination
4. Repetitive movement improves memory skills
5. Teaches relationships between objects
6. Improves visual tracking and following skills

Books with Parts Attached by Velcro, Ribbons

1. Teaches vocabulary skills
2. Improves attention and memory skills
3. Teaches concept of in/out
4. Teaches turn-taking
5. Promotes finger dexterity

Maracas, Bells, Tambourines

1. When parent and baby play together, teaches listening and imitation skills
2. Develops auditory awareness
3. Teaches sequencing

Up on Hands and Knees

SKILLS TO BUILD

- Balancing and shifting weight between upper and lower parts of body
- Developing both right and left sides of body
- Increasing strength, stability of shoulders and arms
- Facilitating use of both right and left brain

EQUIPMENT

- Soft toys, musical toys that move, push-button books, inflatable musical piano, ball with toys inside that move, bright patterned fabric, all so large that baby cannot hold them in hand

EXERCISE

- Place your baby on a well-padded surface—bed, sofa, or floor.
- Place one hand on your baby's tummy and your other hand on your baby's bottom.
- Gently rock your baby forward.
- Take care to provide maximum support to help your baby stay up on his hands and knees.
- Read a story, watch a moving toy, or listen to a musical toy.
- Choose only soft toys, so that if your baby goes forward, he won't get bumped.
- Avoid small toys baby can hold, since he needs both hands on the floor.
- For babies with sensitive skin, do this with baby dressed in overalls or soft cotton clothing covering legs/knees.

I Can Crawl

Here is a progress chart you can use to follow your baby's learning skills. If your baby is a preemie or developmentally delayed, some or all of these skills will appear later than they are shown on the chart.

BABY'S LEARNING SKILLS

Month	6	7	8	9	10	11	12
Uncovers a toy she has seen covered up	👣	👣	👣	👣	👣	👣	👣
Bangs blocks/toys together	👣	👣	👣	👣	👣	👣	👣
Picks up small objects and puts them into mouth	👣	👣	👣	👣	👣	👣	👣
Enjoys reciprocal play—for instance, catching and rolling a ball		👣	👣	👣	👣	👣	👣
Repeats gestures (clapping, eye blinking, finger games), imitates gestures (e.g., "Itsy-Bitsy Spider")		👣	👣	👣	👣	👣	👣
Repeats 1- or 2-syllable sounds ("uh-oh" or "ba ba")		👣	👣	👣	👣	👣	👣
Enjoys musical/action toys; repeatedly pushes button or key to initiate action or sound		👣	👣	👣	👣	👣	👣
Produces vowel sounds, some consonants			👣	👣	👣	👣	👣
Stacks rings/blocks			👣	👣	👣	👣	👣

IMPORTANT: Every baby develops differently. These skills can emerge as late as the last time listed on the chart, and still be well within normal limits.

BABY'S ACCOMPLISHMENTS

By the time your baby is at the crawling stage, she'll have these skills:

🖐 I can get into and out of a sitting position independently, and can play in a side-sitting position (with both arms on one side of my body)

🖐 I have consistent, quick balance reactions. If I lose my balance, my arms come forward, sideways, and sometimes backward to protect my head from injury

🖐 I can now stay on my hands and knees, with my knees together, and rock back and forth. In this position, I can lift one hand and play with a toy

🖐 I can get up into a sitting position independently when lying on my back or tummy (this helps both sides of the brain work together)

🖐 I've developed shoulder stability and arm strength by supporting my weight over my arms when crawling (this is the basis for handwriting and other fine motor skills that require shoulder stability)

🖐 I can point to 8 to 10 objects in single-subject pictures (for instance, "ball," "drink," "Mom," "spoon")

🖐 I can respond to the instructions "go" and "stop" when I'm playing with bells or maracas

🖐 I can play with a toy for 5 minutes

"CAN YOU TELL ME WHY...?"

Answers to Questions Parents Often Ask

My baby crawls, but it's more like a military belly-crawl, with his arms bent and his legs wide apart. How can this be fixed?

Practice the "Ride-a-Horsey" and "Towel Crawl" exercises in this chapter. Also, do the "Take a Trip" exercise in chapter 3, holding your baby's legs together while you travel. When you play with your baby, use your own legs to hold your baby's legs together.

When your baby sleeps, put him in a blanket sleeper that will keep him from spreading his legs Also, avoid using very thick diapers, especially cloth ones, that make it difficult for your baby to bring his legs together. If he's still doing a "belly crawl" after another 6 to 8 weeks, consult your doctor.

My baby's arms seem strong. She can support her weight on her arms, but her legs are still spread wide apart and she seems to fall between her legs when I put her in a crawling position.

Playing on her side will help your baby get used to keeping her legs and knees closer together. Also, encourage her to play in a sitting position with her legs together.

Check out how your baby sits. Are her legs widely spread apart? If so, avoid holding and carrying her with her legs apart. When carrying her or holding her on your lap, bring her legs together. The muscles that bring the legs together may need more use—a problem the exercises in this chapter can help correct.

When I place my baby in a standing position, he sags and doesn't take much weight, or he collapses. His feet roll and he's almost standing on his ankles. What should I do?

Have your baby fitted for high-top leather shoes. When you stand him up, place him against a low table, with you directly behind, supporting his bottom and knees. When he's well supported, stand for 30 seconds, watching a toy or singing. Gradually increase by 10 seconds per day. If this doesn't improve within a few weeks, consult your doctor.

My baby's hands are constantly in fists, and it's hard to get her to hold them out flat when she crawls. What should I do?

Encourage your baby to play in her high chair with water, fingerpaint, yogurt, pudding, other soft food, or a soft cloth, to help her grow accustomed to the feeling of open hands. Avoid tiny toys that encourage her to keep her hands closed tightly. Do the "Airplane" exercise in this chapter, to help your baby practice supporting her weight with open hands. Consult with your doctor if your baby is over 4 months of age and still continually keeps her hands fisted.

My baby hops like a frog rather than crawling or moving each leg separately. Should this be corrected?

Depending on your baby's age, the problem may correct itself. Activities that encourage your baby to use her legs separately can help. When diapering your baby, lift one of her legs at a time, and play "This Little Piggy" with the toes on that foot. Also, put socks on her feet and encourage her to try taking the socks off. Check chapter 3 for exercises that will help your baby learn to move each leg independently.

My baby can stay for a few seconds when I put her in a crawling position, but then she collapses and and falls forward on her face. What's the matter?

Usually when a baby falls forward, it's because she lacks arm stability. The "Towel Crawl," "Take a Trip," and "Ride-a-Horsey" exercises will help her develop arm and shoulder strength. Also, when you play with your baby or read to her, place her over your lap sideways, letting her support her weight with her arms.

I'm afraid that crawling will hurt my baby's knees. Is this true?

Some babies do get abrasions, called "rug burns." Put your baby in thick sweatpants or soft cotton overalls when he's learning to crawl, and he won't have a problem.

PARENTS' STORIES

ROBBY

My son Robby wanted to crawl, but he couldn't seem to figure out how! No matter how hard he tried, he couldn't get into the hands-and-knees position necessary for crawling. He sat up well, but he was very cautious. He was afraid to reach very far to one side for a toy, because he didn't want to fall over.

I placed toys on Robby's left or right side, and provided support so he could safely practice reaching for toys on either side. This exercise gave him confidence, taught him to shift his weight, and helped him learn to use both sides of his body. Before long, Robby started to crawl and was braver when he sat up. Now my problem is trying to keep up with him!

EMMY

Emmy could sit all by herself, if someone sat her down. But she couldn't get into a sitting position by herself, and she couldn't get out of a sitting position. So she'd just sit, and sit, and sit. Then she'd whine until I came to rescue her—or else she'd just fall over and cry. I was worried that she'd hurt herself, but I didn't know how to help her.

Diaper time turned out to be an opportunity for me to show Emma how much she could do. When my husband and I diapered Emma, we'd roll her to her side and bring her halfway up to a sitting position, and then wait. If she wanted to get up, she'd have to push up the rest of the way on her arms. Sometimes I had to wait 30 seconds or even a minute. She'd get mad initially, but when she sat up, we rang bells and praised her. We did additional exercises when we diapered and dressed her.

I Can Crawl

After lots of practice, Emmy learned to rotate while sitting, to sit with her arms to the side and play, and to move easily into and out of sitting. Now she's sitting up all by herself, and it's hard to keep her lying down when she's on the changing table! Because of the skills she learned, crawling—which builds on these skills—came easily for her.

I Can Stand Up

By now, your baby is a masterful crawler who can go up or down stairs, or crawl into the kitchen and get into your cupboards. She's also a human vacuum cleaner, and anything she finds on the floor—papers, dog toys, old Cheerios, dust balls—goes right in her mouth. She's "talking" more, too, and can whine or grunt when she wants something. Frequently she'll babble, and even say 2-syllable sounds. She understands about 50 words, and she's learning to point to objects she wants—a major step in her mental development.

Socially, your baby is becoming aware of who is "family" and who isn't. She'll cuddle up with Mom or Dad, while sometimes being standoffish with strangers. This is a normal stage; somewhere between 6 and 10 months of age, most babies form special attachments to familiar people and become unsure of people they don't know well.

At this age, your baby is on the go all the time. Even diapering her is a struggle, because she's determined to wiggle away from your grasp and take off on another adventure. She also wants to be upright, because she's realizing that standing up is great fun.

Once your baby learns to stand, your tabletops will be fair game, so clear off any small objects, ashtrays, fragile knick-knacks, or plants. Also, keep hot coffee, tea, and soup out of your baby's reach. And use the furniture polish sparingly, because your baby's hands will be all over your furniture from now on—and whatever goes on your baby's hands, goes in her mouth.

HOW BABY STANDS UP

Standing is a skill your baby learns gradually. At 4½ to 6 months, most babies can stand when they're placed in a standing position. At some point between 7 and 12 months, they'll learn to pull themselves to a standing position. But while it's fairly easy for babies to stand, it's difficult for them to sit back down. At first, they tend to land with a great "plop!" on their fannies, sometimes scaring themselves.

It's no wonder that standing takes practice. To stand, your baby needs to extend his body, work against gravity, and control his entire body from his head to his feet. That's a lot to master!

Your baby first learns to stand by pulling up against a surface, usually a table, chair, or sofa. He'll probably start by going from sitting to standing. He'll be a little frightened, but also excited, by this new ability and the world it opens up to him.

Although most babies can stand up from a sitting position, many have trouble reversing the process. At first, babies need to learn how to relax their knees and bend to sit back down. In the beginning, you can sit behind your baby or provide a cushion to help with this transition between standing and sitting. Pay attention to your baby's mood: if he starts fussing after a while, it's probably because he's trying to figure out how to relax his knees and hips and sit down again. Lend him a hand before he becomes frustrated and upset.

Keep an eye on your baby's foot and leg positions when he's standing. If his legs are too far apart or too close together, he won't be able to stand up straight. Also, he should be carrying his weight on both feet equally, not all on one foot. Ideally, your baby's legs should be a shoulder's width apart. Make sure his feet are pointed straight ahead, not turned in or out. If your baby always stands on his toes, or if his feet are turned inward or outward, he may have difficulty balancing and may even develop foot deformities. If he stands correctly, he'll avoid these problems—and he'll form good motor patterns that will last his entire life.

Some babies scrunch up their toes, which is normal but makes it difficult for them to stand up. If your baby's toes are clawed, loosen them gently with your fingers. And if he stiffens on his toes or rolls in on his ankles, see the exercises in chapter 8.

Exercises that will help your baby learn to stand include activities that involve coming to standing from sitting, rocking on hands and feet, and playing in a squatting or kneeling position—all prerequisite skills for a safe, secure transition to standing. Another prerequisite, of course, is confidence. That's why the exercises in this chapter are designed both to make your baby stronger, more stable, and more coordinated, and to give him the feeling "I can do this!"

I Can Stand Up

BABY'S SKILLS TO START

Here are the skills your baby will need before beginning the exercises in this chapter:

- 🎲 I can stand against a table, using my hands for support
- 🎲 I can play against a table in a kneeling position, with my knees together
- 🎲 I can pull up into a standing position
- 🎲 I can get into and out of a sitting position by myself when I'm on the floor
- 🎲 I can play in the side-sitting position
- 🎲 I can sit with a straight back
- 🎲 I can crawl
- 🎲 I can rock back and forth and pull up into a kneeling position
- 🎲 When I fall sideways or forward, my arms always come forward to protect my head

EXERCISES

On My Knees

Do this exercise if your baby falls backward or has trouble keeping her legs together. It will help your baby learn to keep her bottom tucked in.

SKILLS TO BUILD
- Keeping knees together and playing in a kneeling position
- Keeping back straight and holding bottom in while playing in a kneeling position
- Improved balance and stability between upper and lower body

EXERCISE
- Place your baby in a kneeling position on a well-padded floor. Place a toy on a low table in front of her. Sit behind her, supporting her bottom and tummy. **Make sure her knees are almost touching, her feet are not twisted, and her toes are not stuck underneath her feet.**

- In the kneeling position, your baby's bottom should be forward and tucked in so that her back is straight. Her bottom should be in line with her shoulders.
- Provide support to your baby's bottom and legs as necessary to keep her bottom tucked and her knees close together.
- Gradually provide less support as your baby is able to play in the kneeling position independently.

Elevator

SKILLS TO BUILD

- Standing up from a sitting position
- Sitting down from a standing position

EXERCISE

- Sit on the floor. Place your baby in a sitting position on your knee, with his legs approximately 6 inches apart.
- Make sure that your baby's feet are flat on the floor (not on tiptoes) and are pointed forward (not turned in or out).
- Encourage your baby to come to a standing position. Provide support at his knees and hips as needed, to prevent him from locking his knees and to

encourage him to tuck his bottom in. If necessary, slowly raise your leg to bring him to a standing position.

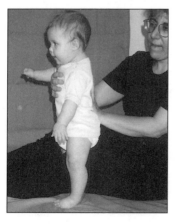

- Once your baby is standing, allow him to balance, while providing support as necessary, to prevent him from falling.
- Provide stability at your baby's hips and encourage him to sit down slowly on your leg.

Stand 'n' Hug

SKILLS TO BUILD

- Developing balance with support
- Becoming comfortable in a standing position
- Standing with bottom tucked in and feet and legs in alignment (feet straight, legs 6 inches apart)

EXERCISE

- Sit on the floor with your legs in a "V" position. Hold your baby close, facing you, and provide support at her hips and upper back so that she is leaning against  you and standing up straight. Make sure that her feet are straight, not rolled in or out at the ankles.
- Place your baby's feet under your legs to keep her from lifting her feet off the floor or rolling on her ankles.
- Encourage your baby to stand up while you provide a big hug for support and security.
- Gradually provide less support as your baby is able to take over.

NOTE: For the baby whose feet are unstable, a high-top shoe will help provide some support. Place your baby in high-top lace-up shoes *only* if your baby's ankles lack stability. Generally, standing a baby barefooted allows you to observe her foot and ankle position easily, and allows her to develop strength and balance in her feet.

Standing Up Tall

SKILLS TO BUILD

- Increased comfort in standing
- Improved standing balance
- Playing in standing position
- Shifting weight from side to side with support

EQUIPMENT

- Low, padded table not to exceed baby's shoulder height, or cardboard box taped to floor
- Interesting toy that moves or plays music, or a book

EXERCISE

- Place your baby against a table in a standing position, feet about 8–10 inches apart.
- Provide support as needed to your baby's bottom and knees to keep him from sagging.
- Stand for 1–2 minutes and read a story, sing a song, or watch a moving/musical toy. Sit directly behind your baby and help him sit down slowly. Don't push this, or do this if your baby is fussy.
- Stay close, sitting beside your baby initially, to prevent him from falling. Be vigilant. Your baby's confidence depends on having a successful standing experience.

Stand against the Wall

SKILLS TO BUILD
- Standing and balancing independently
- Standing with feet, hips, and back in good alignment, feet not turned in or out, and bottom tucked in

EXERCISE

- Place your baby in a standing position with her bottom against the wall. Stand very close, 1–2 inches away, to build baby's confidence and prevent falling.
- Make sure your baby's feet are in alignment and her legs are a shoulder's width apart. Support her knees if they sag, and correct her foot position if she rolls her ankles or turns her feet in or out.
- Play patty-cake or sing songs such as "Itsy-Bitsy Spider" or "Wheels on the Bus."
- Begin standing slowly (30 seconds to a minute at first). Stand very close, so your baby can touch you and use you for support if necessary. Your baby's first experience standing can be very strenuous and tiring. If she seems anxious in this position, sit against the wall beside her and provide support as needed.

On the following page is a progress chart you can use to follow your baby's motor and learning skills. If your baby is a preemie or developmentally delayed, some or all of these skills will appear later than they are shown on the chart.

BABY'S MOTOR SKILLS

MONTH	6	6.5	7	7.5	8	8.5	9	9.5	10	10.5	11	12	13	14	15
Stands supported against a table and plays with a toy			👣	👣	👣	👣	👣	👣	👣	👣	👣	👣	👣	👣	👣
Plays in a kneeling position against a table, with knees together and bottom tucked in				👣	👣	👣	👣	👣	👣	👣	👣	👣	👣	👣	👣
Comes to standing from squat/sitting position				👣	👣	👣	👣	👣	👣	👣	👣	👣	👣	👣	👣
Plays in a squatting position					👣	👣	👣	👣	👣	👣	👣	👣	👣	👣	👣
Pulls up into standing position from sitting or crawling position, using a support					👣	👣	👣	👣	👣	👣	👣	👣	👣	👣	👣
Uses one hand for support while playing in standing position					👣	👣	👣	👣	👣	👣	👣	👣	👣	👣	👣
Bear-walks (pushes up and crawls on hands and feet)						👣	👣	👣	👣	👣	👣	👣	👣	👣	👣
"Cruises" around a table						👣	👣	👣	👣	👣	👣	👣	👣	👣	👣
Lets go of support to pick up a toy or transfer a toy from hand to hand					👣	👣	👣	👣	👣	👣	👣	👣	👣	👣	👣
Stands alone for a few seconds							👣	👣	👣	👣	👣	👣	👣	👣	👣

IMPORTANT: Every baby develops differently. These skills can emerge as late as the last time listed on the chart, and still be well within normal limits.

LEARNING AND PLAYING

At this stage, your baby's getting a better feel for her own body and its relationship to other objects. She also understands spatial concepts; give her a toy that's upside down, for instance, and she'll probably turn it right side up. Her coordination is improving daily, and now she's able to manipulate stacking rings, nesting cups, and large blocks. She can push and pull wheeled toys with strings, and once she learns to stand, she'll be able to push toy shopping carts and lawn mowers.

In addition, your baby is beginning to understand the important mental concepts of anticipation and delayed gratification. Up until this age she's lived in the "now," but she's learning to remember the past and look forward to the future. She knows, too, that she can obtain things she wants by pointing or speaking. She also realizes that objects exist even if she can't see them; for instance, she knows that there's food in the refrigerator and cupboards, and will point to them and say "bottle" or "cracker." Her vocabulary is increasing rapidly, because she understands that language is useful. By reading to your baby regularly, you can teach her new words, as well as help her learn pre-academic skills such as sitting still, paying attention, and following directions.

This is a perfect time to practice imitation, another important skill that will help your baby succeed in school. Have her imitate you clapping hands, waving "bye-bye," brushing teeth and hair, or making animal noises. She'll also enjoy the "yes-no" game, in which she nods "yes" or shakes her head "no" to questions such as "Is this a book?"

I Can Stand Up

- Books that play songs
- Push-button books that match pictures to smaller pictures, using a button
  Baby's Colors
  Friends
  Things That Go
- *Good Night Moon*
- *Dr. Seuss Foot Book*
- *Day at the Park, Visiting Grandma*
- CD-Roms
  Jump Start Toddler
  Reader Rabbit Baby
  Reader Rabbit Toddler

TOY/EQUIPMENT	SKILLS

Sesame Street™
Bop 'N' Boing

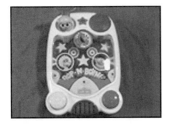

1. Improves eye-hand coordination
2. Develops motor planning
3. Teaches cause-and-effect

Disney™ Musical Stack

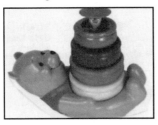

1. Teaches cause/effect
2. Promotes auditory, visual and tactile skills
3. Improves eye/hand coordination
4. Teaches anticipation
5. Teaches spatial relationships

Push-Button Books

1. Teaches cause/effect
2. Helps your baby understand relationships between symbols and language
3. Improves fine motor coordination and fine motor accuracy
4. Helps your baby learn to anticipate events
5. Improves receptive language comprehension and auditory discrimination

I Can Stand Up

Little Tykes™
Rocking Horse

1. Teaches your baby to shift weight forward, backward and sideways
2. Improves balance
3. Teaches spatial orientation
4. Improves tone in abdominal muscles
5. Teaches baby to move hips and upper body separately

See 'N' Say™ Toy

1. Improves finger dexterity
2. Teaches cause-and-effect
3. Improves motor accuracy
4. Teaches memory skills
5. Improves listening skills

Mirror Standing

SKILLS TO BUILD

- Standing without holding parent's hand
- Improved balance
- Learning to use arms while standing up
- Developing arm strength and shoulder stability

EQUIPMENT

- Reusable plastic stickers
- Suction cup toys
- Wall, mirror, or large ball 24–36 inches in diameter
- Can of whipped cream
- Washcloth

EXERCISE

- Place your baby in a standing position, facing away from you (on a well-padded floor).
- Provide support at his hips, making sure his arms are forward, to provide support and balance.
- Check his foot position, making sure his feet are not

turned in or out. His legs should be approximately 4–6 inches apart.

- Play in a standing position, keeping toys or activity at your child's shoulder level. Place the stickers and toys on the mirror, where your baby can reach them, and spray whipped cream on the mirror so he can "finger-paint." Also, let your baby "wash" the mirror with water.

- Sing "finger" songs such as "Itsy-Bitsy Spider" or "Patty-Cake" as baby is able to take hands away.

NOTE: Provide maximum support/supervision to prevent your baby from falling. Your baby must be able to stand against a table independently before doing this exercise.

Here is a progress chart you can use to follow your baby's learning skills. If your baby is a preemie or developmentally delayed, some or all of these skills will appear later than they are shown on the chart.

BABY'S LEARNING SKILLS

MONTH	7	8	9	10	11	12	13	14
Pushes/pulls toy car with string	👣	👣	👣	👣	👣	👣	👣	👣
Activates a toy using switch or push button (e.g., jack-in-the-box. Busybox, or wind-up toy)	👣	👣	👣	👣	👣	👣	👣	👣
Enjoys dumping and filling cups with water	👣	👣	👣	👣	👣	👣	👣	👣
Bangs spoons on pots, bangs on toy drum or piano	👣	👣	👣	👣	👣	👣	👣	👣
Plays with a ball, rolling it back and forth repeatedly	👣	👣	👣	👣	👣	👣	👣	👣
Can put objects in slots		👣	👣	👣	👣	👣	👣	👣
Feeds self Cheerios, bread cubes, crackers		👣	👣	👣	👣	👣	👣	👣

MONTH	7	8	9	10	11	12	13	14
Opens and closes doors	👣	👣	👣	👣	👣	👣	👣	👣
Spatial orientation develops—can tell when something is upside-down		👣		👣	👣	👣	👣	👣
Understands commands/follows simple directions (e.g., "Get your shoes")			👣	👣	👣	👣	👣	👣
Enjoys cause and effect—for instance, likes to turn light switches on and off or make a jack-in-the-box pop up			👣	👣	👣	👣	👣	👣
Pushes walking toy (e.g., shopping cart, toy lawn mower, train)			👣	👣	👣	👣	👣	👣
Imitates animal sounds—cow says "Moo," dog says "Woof"			👣	👣	👣	👣	👣	👣

IMPORTANT: Every baby develops differently. These skills can emerge as late as the last time listed on the chart, and still be well within normal limits.

BABY'S ACCOMPLISHMENTS

When your baby enters the walking stage, she'll be able to show off these skills:

- I can stand up and sit down independently; when I stand, my feet are flat on the floor and pointed forward, my bottom is tucked in, and my legs are 4–6 inches apart

- I can kneel against a table with my bottom tucked in (directly under my shoulders), with my legs and knees together, for at least a minute

- I can crawl up stairs and crawl down backward

- I can stand up for 30 seconds and play "patty-cake"

- I can ride a wheeled toy or rocking horse, balancing with both feet on the floor and using alternating leg movements to propel myself forward

- I understand simple directions (for instance, "Pick up the ball")

- I spend less time putting objects in my mouth, and more time manipulating them with my hands

- I imitate sounds and gestures; for instance, I'll "moo" like a cow, or pretend that I'm driving a car

"CAN YOU TELL ME WHY...?"
Answers to Questions Parents Often Ask

My baby stands on tiptoes. Is that normal?
Occasional tiptoeing is perfectly normal, and helps your baby develop her foot arches. If your baby *always* stands on tiptoe, and has difficulty standing with her feet flat, point this out at your next visit to the doctor. Some babies have tight heel cord muscles, and stand on their tiptoes to keep from falling backward. It's important to intervene before this becomes a habit.

My baby isn't talking—she doesn't say "Mama" or anything.
When you're reading stories to your baby, point at what you're reading. And interact with her while you're reading; for instance, ask her, "Where is the rabbit?," wait until she responds by looking at the picture, and praise her. In addition, show her pictures and then match them to objects around your house. All of these techniques will help her make the connection between words and objects.

Repeat and demonstrate sounds, and encourage your baby to sing sounds, too, such as "E-I-E-I-O" in "Old MacDonald's Farm." Be sure to wait patiently for a response; it may take 1 to 3 minutes for her to react. Repeat any sound your baby makes, and then wait for her to make another sound, so that you're having a "conversation." Also, when your baby wants something, encourage her to ask for it. For instance, if you can see that she wants a cracker, say, "Tell Mom 'cracker,' " and wait. If she makes *any* sound, praise her and give her the cracker.

Studies show that the more you talk and read to your child, the better your child's language skills are likely to be. However, some babies simply talk later than others—and most of the time, there's nothing wrong with the late talkers.

My baby won't take weight; she sags and collapses.
Usually this is characteristic of babies with low muscle tone. The exercises in chapter 4, "I Can Sit Up," will help your baby develop more stable hip and back muscles. Be sure she gets lots of tummy play, too. And play the "standing sandwich" game: place your baby against the wall and face her on your knees, pushing your body against her so she can't sag or fall. Be sure to keep her legs together and her knees straight. Ask your physician if high-top shoes with firm ankle support might help.

If the problem persists, your physician can offer a referral to a therapist. Also consult a doctor if your baby stands mostly on one leg, like a crane; this suggests an imbalance of tone or muscle development that can be improved with therapy.

My baby always wants to hold my hand and doesn't like to stand alone.
Try to help your baby be more comfortable with balance, but don't force her to stand until *she* is ready. The goal is to encourage, not to push. When your baby is able, she'll stand proudly by herself. Some exercises to try include "Stand against the Wall," "Stand 'n' Hug" and "Mirror Standing."

Another trick you can try is "tug–of–war." Using a blanket or towel, hold one end and let your baby pull on the other. Allow your baby to lead in this game, and let her pull you over.

Also, have your baby play two-handed games while standing. For instance, show her how to put plastic cards into an oatmeal box with a slot in the top. When her hands are busy and her brain is occupied with mastering this game, she may not realize that she's standing by herself!

My baby seems very active. He is forever pulling toys down from shelves, and opening and closing doors. Is my baby hyperactive?

Your baby is probably an active, normal toddler. Most babies have a 3 to 5 minute attention span for toys or stories they really like. Activities such as pulling toys down from shelves or opening and closing doors are exploration, not hyperactivity.

However, it's important to structure a "busy" baby's activities. Encourage your baby to play with a toy for at least three to five minutes, gradually increasing the time, and limit the number of toys you give him; otherwise, he may be overwhelmed. Change toys every few weeks, rather than putting them all out at once. Give baby a drawer or shelf for toys, so he can take them out and afterward put them back.

PARENTS' STORIES

MEGAN

Megan couldn't or wouldn't stand up. All of our friends' babies could stand with a little help, but Megan just sagged and collapsed when I stood her up. When she lay on her back, her legs turned out like a frog's. I also noticed that she didn't bend her knees to her chest like most babies.

We used several approaches to help Megan overcome her problem. First, we bought her firm, high-top walking shoes. Just having a stable base for support helped a lot. Second, when I diapered Megan, I put bracelets, wrist rattles, and socks on her feet. That encouraged her to practice lifting her legs, helping to bring her legs together and build up her tummy muscles. We played a lot while kneeling against a low hassock, and we even watched Barney *together while kneeling. I supported her knees at first, and gradually she took over. Once Megan developed better muscle tone, and learned to stabilize herself on her new shoes, she found out that standing was easy and fun.*

JASON

Jason was a busy guy, always into everything. I was constantly saying "no" to him, and my mother-in-law kept telling me to slap his hands when he caused trouble. He tried to put a fork in an electric socket, unrolled all the toilet paper, and threw his cars in the potty when I went to get the mail. He didn't sit still for long, even for the story sessions that enthralled the other children in his baby class.

I didn't think it was right to punish Jason for being an active, adventurous boy. Instead, I covered the electrical outlets, kept the bathroom doors closed, and bought "potty locks" to keep him out of the toilets. Then I bought a low slide and a safe climbing toy, and put them in the family room so Jason could wear himself out safely. I also scheduled two 5-minute reading sessions each day, to help Jason learn to sit still and pay attention. When he tried to get up, I'd say, "Just one more minute," and give him a toy to keep him entertained while I read to him.

Now Jason uses up his excess energy playing on his indoor playground, and he's gradually learning to sit quietly for longer periods of time. He's still an on-the-go kid, but he's a lot less busy than before! And he has a much longer attention span, so he enjoys our reading sessions—especially when he can "help out" by turning pages and pointing.

Chapter Seven

I Can Walk

Happy First Birthday! Your baby is almost a toddler now, and he's getting more independent every day. He's standing and walking while holding your hand, and he can say single words. He also can pull himself up to a standing position and then sit down again, holding on to furniture.

Your baby isn't putting everything in his mouth anymore; he's more sophisticated now, and prefers to manipulate his toys. He knows what he wants, and demands objects by pointing to them. If he's hungry, he may go to the refrigerator. When he's finished eating, he'll say "down" or "done," or throw his food or his plate. He loves to fill cups or buckets with sand or water, and then dump them out.

At some point around this age—although it might be as

early as 8 months or as late as 18 months—your child will take that first real "baby step." What a thrilling accomplishment! Walking opens up a whole new world for your baby, and it's an exciting stage for proud parents as well. Every child has a different time line for walking, but you can provide exercises that develop balance and muscle tone so that your baby can walk with skill and confidence.

Some babies are hesitant to walk, and need a little gentle encouragement to take those first steps. Here's some advice: rather than "walking" your baby by holding his upraised arms, encourage him to ride a wheeled toy or push a chair across the floor. This develops independence and self-confidence, and gives your toddler the idea "Maybe I can do this on my own." Also, some babies have sensitive feet, and may be reluctant to walk for this reason. If your baby doesn't like having the soles of his feet touched, help him get accustomed to this sensation by encouraging him to stand and crawl on a carpet or in grass or sand. Also, play foot games such as "This Little Piggy," rub his feet with a towel, or encourage him to play games that involve pushing his heels against the floor.

Be patient, however, if your baby is content to crawl for a few more weeks. Walking shouldn't be rushed, and your baby isn't wasting time while he's crawling; he's learning these skills that he'll need to walk well:

1. Balance: Your baby must be able to balance automatically and return to a straight-up position when his weight is shifted sideways, forward, or backward. He'll need to be able to adjust to changes in position smoothly and quickly.
2. Alignment: To walk, your baby must keep his back straight, his bottom tucked in, his head, shoulders, and hips in alignment, and his feet a shoulder-span apart.
3. Weight-shifting: Your baby must be able to pick up one leg, shift all his weight to the opposite side of his body, and still stay upright.

4. Protective reactions: Your baby is continuing to refine these reactions, which allow him to use his arms quickly and consistently to catch himself and protect himself from injury.

These skills will develop at different times for different children. Prepare your child with the exercises that follow, and then be patient—it'll happen. And be sure to keep film in your camera, so you'll be ready to capture those first steps for posterity!

I Can Walk

BABY'S SKILLS TO START

Before doing the exercises in this chapter, your baby should have the following skills:

- 🎲 I can "cruise" around a table, holding on intermittently for support, and can let go and stand up without support for 5 seconds independently
- 🎲 I can stand with my feet flat and straight (not turned in or out, or rolled at the ankles), my bottom tucked in, and my legs a shoulder-width apart, and pick up an object from the floor
- 🎲 I can walk a short distance while holding a grown-up's hand
- 🎲 I can stand with my feet on the floor, flat and forward
- 🎲 I can stand straight without sagging at my knees
- 🎲 I can sit down from a standing position
- 🎲 I can stand up from a sitting position independently
- 🎲 I can play in a squatting position

NOTE: Don't let your baby fall during these exercises that follow. This is a time when his confidence is developing, and a fall could make him fearful.

EXERCISES

One Leg Up: Cruising

SKILLS TO BUILD
- Walking sideways
- Lifting foot and stepping over objects, in preparation for walking

EQUIPMENT
- Low table
- Small pillow or bolster (3 to 4 inches wide)
- Toy

EXERCISE
- Begin with your baby standing at a low table. While sitting behind your baby, support her bottom with one hand. Make sure her legs are a shoulder-width apart and her feet are point-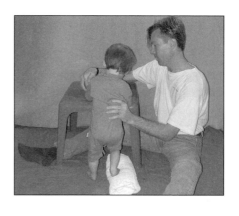ed forward, not rolled in. Place the pillow or bolster between your baby's legs.
- Place a toy on the table 3 to 6 inches to one side of your baby, so she has to take one step to the side, stepping over the pillow or bolster, to get the toy. Gradually lift your baby's leg, if she needs help to do this at first.
- Let your baby play with the toy for a minute, then move the toy to the other side of your baby, and repeat.

Push the Chair

SKILLS TO BUILD

- Keeping weight forward
- Keeping arms forward. This will help your baby to protect her head if her balance is upset

EQUIPMENT

- Low chair, stool with wheels, or large rubber ball

EXERCISE

- Place your baby in a standing position against a chair, stool, or large ball. Sit next to her and make sure she's standing upright with her feet straight and her legs a shoulder-width apart.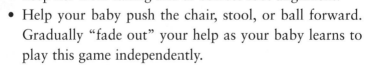
- Stay close to your baby and provide support as necessary to keep her from falling and to correct foot alignment.
- Help your baby push the chair, stool, or ball forward. Gradually "fade out" your help as your baby learns to play this game independently.

TIP: For children who are small and weigh less, a cardboard box substitutes well for a chair.

TIP: You can check your baby's foot alignment best if she is barefooted. However, if your baby has weak ankles or her feet roll in or out, provide her with a fairly firm shoe with good arch support for these exercises.

Step Start

SKILLS TO BUILD

- Becoming comfortable with one foot forward, one foot back (necessary for walking)
- Practicing shifting weight forward and keeping bottom tucked in

EQUIPMENT

- Wall for support

EXERCISE

- Stand 1–2 inches in front or to the side of your baby.
- Place your baby in a standing position with his bottom against the wall for support.
- Provide support to your baby's side.

- Gently bring one of your baby's legs forward while his back leg stays behind. His feet should be 3–4 inches apart.
- Stand for 3–5 seconds; increase to 30 seconds. Sing a song—"Old MacDonald"/"Wheels on the Bus."

NOTE: In this exercise, the back leg takes almost all of your baby's weight, so support that side (e.g., if his left leg is back, support his left side).

Kick the Ball

SKILLS TO BUILD

- Lifting one leg while standing upright on the other leg, to prepare for walking
- Developing refined balance reactions in feet

EQUIPMENT

- Open wall space/well-padded or carpeted floor
- Light plastic ball, 12–16 inches in diameter

EXERCISE

- Place your baby in a standing position with her bottom against the wall. Make sure that her legs are a shoulder-span apart, and that her feet are forward and not rolled in or out.
- Sit next to your baby and be sure to **provide support to the knee and hip of the leg your baby will not be using to kick,** to keep this leg straight so that she doesn't fall when the kicking leg is lifted.
- Place the ball directly against the toe of your baby's foot.
- Encourage your baby to kick, using her right leg and standing on her left leg.
- Repeat, having your baby kick with her left leg and stand on her right leg.

Standing Up Tall

SKILLS TO BUILD
- Shifting weight and balancing in standing position
- Lifting one leg and staying upright when being dressed

EQUIPMENT
- Baby's clothes, ready to put on

EXERCISE
- Place your baby in a standing position. Stand or sit behind him, or use a wall to provide support and stability as necesary. Your baby's feet and legs should be straight and not more than 6 inches apart.

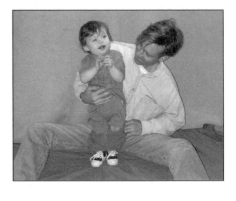

- Encourage your baby to remain standing while being dressed. When putting on his shirt, bring the shirt forward so that your baby's head comes forward (rather than going backward). Encourage your baby to lift his legs for pants and socks as he becomes more secure.

Here is a progress chart you can use to follow your baby's motor development. If your baby is a preemie or developmentally delayed, some or all of these skills will appear later than they are shown on the chart.

BABY'S MOTOR SKILLS

Month	9	9.5	10	10.5	11	11.5	12	12.5	13	13.5	14	14.5	15
Stands against a ball or chair	👣	👣	👣	👣	👣	👣	👣	👣	👣	👣	👣	👣	👣
Pushes a chair around the room		👣	👣	👣	👣	👣	👣	👣	👣	👣	👣	👣	👣
Lifts leg to sidestep an object when cruising around furniture		👣	👣	👣	👣	👣	👣	👣	👣	👣	👣	👣	👣
Lifts toes when tilted backward			👣	👣	👣	👣	👣	👣	👣	👣	👣	👣	👣
Stands and pushes a large ball away, stands alone and plays catch				👣	👣	👣	👣	👣	👣	👣	👣	👣	👣
Rolls onto tiptoes when tilted gently forward				👣	👣	👣	👣	👣	👣	👣	👣	👣	👣
Will lift leg and kick a ball when standing against a wall					👣	👣	👣	👣	👣	👣	👣	👣	👣
Walks while holding parent's hand					👣	👣	👣	👣	👣	👣	👣	👣	👣

Month	9	9.5	10	10.5	11	11.5	12	12.5	13	13.5	14	14.5	15
Stands with one foot forward, one foot back					👣	👣	👣	👣	👣	👣	👣	👣	👣
Walks a short distance (1 to 2 steps) between furniture						👣	👣	👣	👣	👣	👣	👣	👣
Stands independently and maintains balance while being dressed							👣	👣	👣	👣	👣	👣	👣
Will take a step forward or backward to maintain balance							👣	👣	👣	👣	👣	👣	👣

IMPORTANT: Every baby develops differently. These skills can emerge as late as the last time listed on the chart, and still be well within normal limits.

I Can Walk

LEARNING AND PLAYING

Your 1-year-old loves to hide from Mommy or Daddy, roll a ball back and forth with another person, and imitate gestures and sounds. She also enjoys playing independently with toys, or household objects such as pots and pans. She understands simple directions; for example, you can tell her to get her shoes and she'll follow through. Ideal games at this stage are patty-cake, peek-a-boo, stacking and knocking over blocks, turning light switches on and off, and opening and shutting doors. She's mastering concepts such as in/out, up/down, near/far, open/close, so introduce them into games and reading sessions whenever you can.

By reading to your 1-year-old, you'll help her develop an understanding of verbs, begin teaching her to classify and categorize objects (for instance, "things to eat" and "things that go"), and introduce her to concepts such as size and same/different (for instance, big/little, hot/cold, soft/hard, wet/dry). Reading also gives her an opportunity to practice her listening and memory skills.

BEST BOOKS FOR THIS AGE

- Books that play familiar songs
- Heavy plastic reusable sticker books
- Push-button books, such as *Baby's Colors*, *Things That Go*, and *Animals at the Farm*, which teach babies to analyze similarities and differences
- Computer programs such as *Jump Start Toddler* and *Reader Rabbit Toddler*. Even at this age, your baby can use a computer mouse or "easy ball" to find hidden pictures or pop bubbles in a computer reading game—an excellent way to introduce the concept of cause-and-effect.

TOY/EQUIPMENT SKILL

**Toddler Train Push Toy
with Walker Handle**

1. Teaches baby to move legs separately
2. Improves balance and equilibrium
3. Develops foot arches and balance reactions in feet
4. Improves depth perception and motor planning

School Bus with People

1. Teaches spatial relationships
2. Improves eye/hand coordination
3. Encourages imitation skills
4. Teaches concepts of forward/backward, on/off, open/close, in/out

Inflatable Bopper

1. Teaches cause-and-effect
2. Improves balance and equilibrium
3. Fun to tackle and push
4. Improves eye/hand coordination and motor planning

I Can Walk

Duck Roller

1. Increases strength of large muscles, expecially shoulders, arms, and hips
2. Improves balance and equilibrium
3. Develops foot arch and foot alignment
4. Teaches motor planning skills—baby learns muscle movements needed to make the duck move

Jump Start Toddler

1. Enhances auditory memory and attention span
2. Teaches object permanence (an object is still present even if baby can't see it)
3. Teaches early matching skills
4. Teaches "figure-ground" discrimination—baby learns to identify individual objects in pictures

Reader Rabbit Toddler

1. Enhances auditory memory
2. Teaches cause-and-effect
3. Teaches spatial concepts
4. Improves eye/hand coordination and motor accuracy
5. Promotes visual skills, color recognition

Shopping Trip

SKILLS TO BUILD
- Standing independently
- Standing with arms forward to protect head in case balance is upset
- Pushing a toy forward while standing

EQUIPMENT
- Toy grocery cart (a cardboard box also works, or a big walk-and-push toy with handle)
- Telephone book inside the cart or box, for stability, at first
- Teddy, doll, or favorite toys

EXERCISE
- Place your baby in a standing position in front of the cart or cardboard box. Provide as much support as she needs, for stability.
- Once your baby is comfortable standing against the cart, let her stand independently.

- Encourage your baby to put toys into the cart and push the cart forward and backward.
- Explore (1) pushing the cart around the room; (2) placing the cart against the wall for additional stability if your baby seems fearful.

NOTE: Do this exercise only if your baby has fairly good balance when standing.

Here is a progress chart you can use to follow your baby's learning development. If your baby is a preemie or developmentally delayed, some or all of these skills will appear later than they are shown on the chart.

BABY'S LEARNING SKILLS

Month	9	9.5	10	10.5	11	11.5	12	12.5	13	13.5	14	14.5	15
Enjoys pushing large toys or boxes around room	👣	👣	👣	👣	👣	👣	👣	👣	👣	👣	👣	👣	👣
Enjoys opening/shutting doors, drawers, etc.		👣	👣	👣	👣	👣	👣	👣	👣	👣	👣	👣	👣
Enjoys hiding behind doors	👣	👣	👣	👣	👣	👣	👣	👣	👣	👣	👣	👣	👣
Explores sound and rhythm, plays drums, shakes noisemaker	👣	👣	👣	👣	👣	👣	👣	👣	👣	👣	👣	👣	👣
Points to body parts—nose, hair, tummy, toes		👣	👣	👣	👣	👣	👣	👣	👣	👣	👣	👣	👣
Understands "stop/go"				👣	👣	👣	👣	👣	👣	👣	👣	👣	👣
Rides low or 3-wheeled toy					👣	👣	👣	👣	👣	👣	👣	👣	👣
Builds towers of 2 or more blocks							👣	👣	👣	👣	👣	👣	👣

BABY'S LEARNING SKILLS (CONTINUED)

Month	9	9.5	10	10.5	11	11.5	12	12.5	13	13.5	14	14.5	15
Plays Peek-a-Boo, "Itsy-Bitsy Spider," "Wheels on the Bus" upon demonstration or request							👣	👣	👣	👣	👣	👣	👣
Enjoys 2-step activities (e.g., feeding and washing doll, loading and dumping truck)				👣	👣	👣	👣	👣	👣	👣	👣	👣	👣
Says first sound of words ("bub" for bubble, "da" for Dad, "ga" for go)				👣	👣	👣	👣	👣	👣	👣	👣	👣	👣
Imitates nods (for yes) and head shakes (for no), waves "bye-bye"							👣	👣	👣	👣	👣	👣	👣

IMPORTANT: Every baby develops differently. These skills can emerge as late as the last time listed on the chart, and still be well within normal limits.

Baby's Accomplishments

At the walking stage, your baby will be able to show off these new skills:

🖐 I can stand with my bottom against the wall and one foot in front of the other; I can lift one leg up off the floor and kick a ball

🖐 When I'm tilted back as I'm standing, I can tuck my chin, keep my arms forward, and tilt my feet up to maintain my balance

🖐 I can be dressed in a standing position with very little support

🖐 I can lift one leg sideways while my other leg and knee provide support and stability. I can walk sideways along a wall unaided

🖐 While standing, I can squat down to the floor, pick up a toy, and place it in a container at waist height

🖐 I can understand about 50 to 100 of the words Mommy uses

🖐 I can match objects to pictures (show me a picture of a chair, for instance, and I can show you a real chair)

🖐 I understand the meaning of opposites such as hot/cold, big/little, on/off, up/down

🖐 I can follow simple 2-step directions (for instance, "Get your shoes and your socks"), and I can imitate a 2- to 3-step sequence in finger games or singing games

"CAN YOU TELL ME WHY...?"

Answers to Questions Parents Often Ask

My baby can stand, and walks when we hold her hand, but she won't walk on her own; she cries or sits down.
Babies walk only when they have sufficient balance and strength, and have developed good "protective reactions" so they can catch themselves if they lose their balance. Give her time to develop these skills. Encourage her to ride or push a riding toy; this will help her develop more confidence and balance. Also, play games in which you and your baby hold on to a push-toy and walk together. Or stand very close to her, and encourage her to take just one step toward you.

While it's a good idea to encourage your baby to walk, don't push her. Some babies are in a bigger hurry than others! It's normal for babies to learn to walk at any age from 8 to 18 months. Have your baby's doctor examine her to make sure she doesn't have any physical problems that could delay walking.

My baby climbs, and I am concerned about the danger, particularly when he climbs on the windowsill or on the tables. What can I do besides say "no-no?"
Some babies, particularly boys, seem driven to climb. If possible, put a low climber (or a slide with an enclosed upper area) in your family room or a bedroom, so your baby gets a chance to climb several times a day. Or you can stack sofa or bed pillows on a soft surface and let your baby go at it.

Try to avoid saying "No!" when your baby climbs. Instead, say "Stop," or "Danger." Then offer a safe alternative. For instance, give your baby a cardboard box with a door cut into it, and ask him, "Can you climb into this?" Or let him climb on a low hassock or a cloth mattress. (Don't use a plastic air mattress, bean-bag chair, or beanbag pillow; babies can suffocate on these.)

My baby isn't saying any words. To show me what she wants, she grunts, points, or pulls on me. How can I encourage her to talk? We're both getting frustrated.
Make a small picture book of her favorite toys, pets, foods, and people. (Either cut pictures out of magazines, or use photos.) Read the book together and ask her questions—for instance, "Here's kitty. What's this?" Wait patiently for her to answer (it may take a few minutes), and when she makes any attempt to speak, reward her with praise.

Also, when she grunts in an attempt to obtain a desired object, pretend that you don't understand her. Say, "Try again—I don't know what you're saying." If she asks even a *little* more clearly the second time, give her the item she wants. (Do this only with a few items at first, so she doesn't get too frustrated.)

My baby walks easily around a table but can't walk on her own. Why?
Your baby can stand against a table without having to shift her weight sideways and backward. In order to walk alone, she must be able to keep her bottom tucked in and maintain her balance while moving forward and backward. Most babies stand against a table and "cruise" for at least 2 to 3 months before learning to walk alone.

PARENTS' STORIES

CARTER

I knew Carter could walk on his own, if he'd just let go of my hand. I was tired of carrying him—after all, he was almost a year old, and getting BIG! For three whole months he'd been holding my hand while he walked.

I played games with Carter that involved standing against the wall and putting objects into containers using two hands. We also played the "horsey" game, in which I was the horse and Carter used ribbons as "reins" to pull me. Then I'd let the ribbons go, and say, "I dropped the reins!" Carter was so intrigued by the game that he wouldn't realize that he was standing by himself. These games helped him gain confidence.

After taking a step to kick a ball during another exercise, Carter discovered he could take steps alone, and—finally— he began to walk all by himself. I don't know which one of us was more excited!

RACHEL

Rachel could stand up on her own when she was 6 months old. Now she was 14 months old, and she'd stand against the coffee table and play for 15 minutes at a time. She'd walk while holding someone's hand, but she wouldn't walk on her own. When we tried to let go of her hand, she would cry or sit down. We felt she was ready to walk, but she needed a jump start.

The "Stand against the Wall" exercise (chapter 6) turned out to be just the help Rachel needed. We played patty-cake, peek-a-boo, and "Itsy-Bitsy Spider" while she stood against the wall, and she had a wonderful time while simultaneous-

ly becoming more confident. The "Stand 'n' Hug" exercise (chapter 6) also encouraged Rachel to stand alone with intermittent support. We bought her a toy shopping cart and encouraged her to grab boxes from shelves and put them in her cart, and often she'd get so busy "shopping" that she'd forget to hang on to the cart. In a few weeks, she developed the confidence and independence she needed to walk on her own.

Feet, Feet, Feet

Why a special chapter about feet? Because strong, straight feet help your baby crawl, stand, and walk correctly. Furthermore, your baby's early foot development can set the stage for a lifetime of healthy feet—or a lifetime of foot, leg, and back problems.

Your child can stand and walk much more comfortably, and with greater endurance, if her feet are correctly aligned and she has strong foot arches to support her ankles. Good foot stability and alignment also can help protect her from back and hip problems as an adult. And whether she wants to learn ballet, play basketball, or take up tennis, her agility and coordination when she's older will depend in part on how strong and well-developed her feet are.

Right now, your baby is working hard on developing her foot muscles. She has her work cut out for her, because each foot has 19 muscles, and there are 12 more muscles running from her lower leg to her foot. She'll exercise these muscles all day, by rolling, pounding her heels against the floor, lifting her fanny off the floor with her legs, and playing with her feet. Another excellent way for her to exercise all of those muscles, of course, is to stand and walk on them.

SHOES—OR NO SHOES?

Most babies learn to stand and walk while barefooted. This provides sensory feedback to their feet, gives the foot muscles a better workout, develops balance reactions, and helps babies grow accustomed to the feel of different surfaces—carpet, floor, grass, and so on. I recommend skipping socks, too, unless it's cold; in addition to reducing the range of motion in your baby's feet and interfering with her balance, they can be slippery and dangerous on uncarpeted floors. Of course, your baby will need shoes for foot protection when she's outdoors. A soft, flexible shoe that allows for air exchange—not a shoe made of plastic—is best.

If your child's ankles roll inward when she stands, however, a good shoe is called for. Purchase a firm, well-fitted, high-top shoe that will help provide foot support and stability, and will prevent your child from overstretching her ankle joints. Make sure you buy the correct width of shoe (have it measured), and be sure the heel and ankle portions of the shoe are firm and well fitted. Don't buy shoes that are too large; the extra width can cause your baby's foot to roll inside the shoe.

There are no special shoes available for the child whose feet turn in or out, but you can help correct this problem by having your child practice standing and walking with her feet in alignment. If one of your baby's feet turns out, have your baby walk in circles with that foot on the outside of the circle. If one foot turns in, have your baby walk in circles with that foot on the inside of the circle. You can also have your baby practice walking on a path marked by parallel blocks.

A very few babies need some extra help in the form of shoe inserts. These special inserts require a doctor's prescription, and may be covered by your insurance plan. They control too-high or too-low tone in the foot, and can help prevent foot deformity or overstretching.

Occasional tiptoeing is normal, but babies who tiptoe most or all of the time may have problems ranging from tight heel cords to hypersensitivity. Excessive tiptoeing usually is fairly easy to resolve with stretching or desensitization exercises. If your baby walks on her tiptoes more than 25 percent of the time, your doctor can refer you to specialists who can determine the causes and proper treatment of her tiptoeing.

FOOT ALIGNMENT

Check out your baby's foot alignment. When your baby is sitting, lying on his back, or standing, how are his feet positioned? Are both feet always turned widely in or out? Does one foot always seem to turn in? Does he always "claw" his feet, gripping with his toes for balance when he stands?

Babies just beginning to walk often will toe in or out with one or both feet. Many will also claw their feet occasionally. As they become more comfortable with standing and walking, and develop better balance, most outgrow these habits. However, some children need extra help learning to stand and walk with their feet in alignment.

To determine whether or not your baby has good foot alignment, use this checklist:

Your baby's feet should be in alignment most of the time, not turned in or out.

Your baby should stand on flat feet most of the time, not up on his toes.

Your baby should be able to stand without locking his knees, with his legs a shoulder-width apart.

Your child's feet should not roll in at the ankles.

Occasional toe clawing is normal, but your baby's toes should not always be clawed.

If you detect problems, point them out to your doctor. (Don't expect the doctor to spot these problems without your input, because he or she isn't likely to see your baby standing for any significant length of time.) The doctor can let you know if intervention might be helpful.

The exercises in this chapter aren't a substitute for professional intervention, but they can strengthen your baby's foot and ankle muscles, correct toe clawing, and possibly prevent flat feet, pigeon toes, and foot deformities from developing.

EXERCISES

Bridge Up

In addition to developing your baby's hip and bottom muscles, this exercise will help strengthen his feet and help develop his balance reactions. If your child's feet turn in or out, this is a good exercise to do.

SKILLS TO BUILD
- Developing the muscles your baby uses to balance with his feet
- Developing foot arches
- Developing tolerance to supporting weight on feet
- Supporting weight with feet in good alignment

EXERCISE
- Place your baby on his back with his head centered.
- Bring your baby's knees together, and place his feet on the floor with his heels and feet straight.

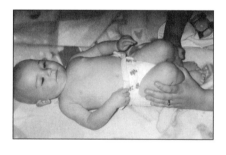

Provide stability as needed until your baby is able to hold his knees together independently for a few seconds.
- Gently push down on your baby's legs for 5 seconds, so he can experience the feeling of supporting his weight with his feet in good alignment.
- Pick up your baby's feet one at a time. Also, encourage your baby to pick up one foot at a time. (Stroking him behind the knee, or stroking the leg you want him to lift, will encourage your baby to lift his leg.)

Brush My Feet

SKILLS TO BUILD

- Keeping foot straight

EQUIPMENT

- Soft baby hairbrush (optional)

EXERCISE

- With your baby in your lap, facing forward, use one hand to hold his leg, providing support at his ankle. Make sure that his leg is pointed forward, not turned in or out.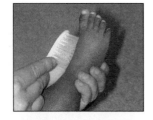

- If your baby's **foot turns out**, use your thumb, index finger, or a soft baby hairbrush to stroke the inner border of his foot. Start at the top of your baby's big toe, and continue down to his inner heel. Once your baby's foot is in alignment, hold the position so that he grows accustomed to the feeling of his foot in alignment.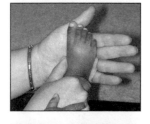

- If your baby's **foot turns in**, stroke the outer border of his foot, starting just behind the little toe, and continuing down to his outer heel. Once your baby's foot is in alignment, hold the position so that he grows accustomed to the feeling of his foot in alignment.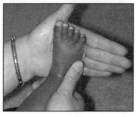

NOTE: Avoid brushing or pushing against any portion of the bottom of baby's foot.

Side-Stepping

Do this exercise if your baby's feet turn in or out.

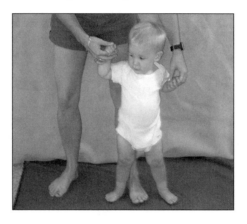

SKILLS TO BUILD
- Straightening feet and walking with feet in alignment

EXERCISE
- Place your baby in a standing position. Hold her hand for support, and place your foot between her feet.
- Have your baby walk around a table, taking sideways steps rather than stepping forward or backward. If your baby's right foot turns **out**, encourage her to side-step to the left; if her left foot turns **out**, side-step to the right. Use your foot to guide her foot into alignment.
- If your baby's right foot turns **in**, encourage her to side-step to the right. If her left foot turns **in**, encourage her to side-step to the left. Use your foot to guide your baby's foot into alignment.

Foot Games

SKILLS TO BUILD

- Walking with good foot position
- Taking weight equally over both feet
- Keeping feet straight
- Improving balance and foot stability

EQUIPMENT

- Indoor floor free of obstacles or toys

EXERCISE

- Stand to one side of your baby and hold his hand.
- Walk in a circle about 36 to 48 inches in diameter. The smaller the circle, the more your baby must turn his feet.
- Gently hold your baby's hand. Do not pull.
- If your baby cries, do not do this exercise. It should be fun.
- Provide support to keep your baby from tripping over his own feet.

If baby's right foot turns in, walk clockwise in circle.

If baby's right foot turns out, walk counterclockwise in circle.

If baby's left foot turns in, walk counterclockwise in circle.

If baby's left foot turns out, walk clockwise in circle.

Rocking Horse

SKILLS TO BUILD

- Keeping arms up and forward to protect against head injury
- Shifting weight forward and backward
- Putting weight on feet with good foot alignment
- Exploring cause-and-effect and position in space

EQUIPMENT

- Low rocking horse
- Well-padded floor

EXERCISE

- Place your baby on the seat of the rocking horse. Place her hands on the handles.
- Provide support as necessary to keep your baby from falling off. You may need to hold her feet on the stirrups at first.
- Be aware of your baby's foot position. Place your baby's feet so she can rock with her feet straight.
- If your baby turns one foot in or out, realign/support as needed, to encourage her to practice taking weight with good foot position.
- Wait for your baby to explore moving forward and backward, then move the horse as needed to help your baby learn to rock.
- Rock the horse a few inches if your baby is hesitant.

"CAN YOU TELL ME WHY...?"
Answers to Questions Parents Often Ask

My baby is very flexible, and loves to put his feet in his mouth. He is five months old. Is this okay?

Yes! Lots of babies do this. It's a wonderful and gentle stretching exercise, and helps develop foot mobility that can later be helpful in ballet, soccer, or other activities requiring fancy footwork, flexibility, and good range of motion.

My baby loves to stand on my lap, and seems happiest when she's upright. Is it all right for her to stand, even though she's only a few months old?

It's fine to let your baby stand on your lap, but she also needs plenty of floor time so she can learn to roll and crawl. Also, even at this early age, be aware of your baby's foot position when she stands. She's developing sensory motor patterns for later independent standing, so make sure her feet are in good alignment. If she stands on her toes, encourage her to stand with her feet flat.

What should I put on my baby's feet to prevent her from slipping and still keep her feet warm?

Slipper sox with rubber bottoms provide great stability and reduce your baby's chances of slipping. They're cozy, warm, and inexpensive, and protect your baby's feet while allowing her freedom of movement.

Special Babies, Special Parents

If you are the parent of a special-needs baby, you'll soon discover a surprising secret: these babies are treasures, not tragedies. I've worked with hundreds of parents of special-needs babies over the past 20 years, and these parents continually tell me about the great joy that their children bring them. As one parent of a special-needs baby put it, "You have been given a child of immense worth, who has so much to teach you."

You also find out that you're not alone, because more than 300,000 special-needs babies are born each year in the United States. While parents of special-needs babies once felt isolated, now it's easy to find other parents with the same concerns and needs as you.

As an expert in working with special-needs children, my best advice is: Network! Get connected. Find organizations of parents with special-needs children. Talk to your local health department, children's hospital, or developmental center. You'll be amazed at the wealth of resources in your community, and at the number of people—teachers, therapists, public health nurses, other parents—who can help you. If you have a computer, you'll find that it's easy to search out on-line information on parent groups, medical facilities, and educational and recreational programs.

You'll also be surprised at how much your baby is capable of learning and doing. With early intervention, including therapy and education, special-needs babies can make remarkable strides. The large majority of preemies, and many mildly delayed babies, will catch up to their peers. And children with more significant disabilities, once confined to restrictive lives, now lead full, active, productive, and happy lives in their communities.

You can help your special-needs baby maximize his potential by seeking out quality schools and therapy programs with high levels of expertise. The first step I recommend is to find a doctor knowledgeable about special-needs infants. (Parent groups can be a huge help in recommending physicians.) Also, arrange for an evaluation by a therapist who is N.D.T. (neurodevelopmental therapy) trained. This is a graduate training course taken after a therapist has become licensed, so an N.D.T. therapist is a real expert.

Your child's doctors and therapists can help you design an individualized therapy program for his individual needs. But your baby has another important expert in his corner, and that's you. Nobody knows your infant's skills, needs, and interests better than you, and no one will be more dedicated to helping your child achieve his potential.

The exercises and advice in this chapter can help, by supplementing your child's therapy program. Check with your baby's therapist, who can give you advice on which of the exercises and activities in this chapter, and in the other chapters of this book, will be most helpful for your child. Every child is unique, and exercises that work for one baby may not work for another. (While I use the term "baby," there's no age limit for these exercises. Every special child develops on a different timetable, and some will benefit from these exercises at 6 months while others will be ready at 8 months or a year—or even later.)

If your baby has health problems that might make exercising a concern, be sure to consult with your physician before doing any of the exercises in this book. Also, when you're working out with your baby, read his cues. If he's fussy and upset, the activity is probably too much for him. If he's having a great time, you're on the right track!

You'll notice that this chapter doesn't discuss specific medical conditions other than prematurity. That's because the exercises and activities in each section will benefit babies with a wide range of diagnoses. I've divided this chapter into 5 sections, each one focusing on a different type of pattern commonly seen in special-needs babies. The sections are:

- Preemies
- High-need babies
- Babies who exhibit asymmetry
- Babies with low muscle tone
- Babies with delayed development

If your baby doesn't fit neatly into one of these categories, ask your pediatrician or therapist which exercises and activities will help him the most. And remember, playing and bonding with your baby are as important as teaching new skills. The activities and exercises I'll suggest all have therapeutic value, but they're also "child's play"—so have fun!

PREEMIES

If your baby's a preemie (a baby born prematurely, after less than 37 weeks), you're probably feeling two distinctly different emotions: joy that your baby is coming home, and trepidation about the special care he'll need.

Your baby may require a feeding tube or supplemental oxygen, and may be sensitive, difficult to calm, and jittery. In addition, he'll look different from other babies for a while, until he catches up. It's normal to feel overwhelmed by your preemie's special needs, and even to be alarmed by his appearance. But be patient! In a few months, your preemie will put on weight, start sleeping better, and probably be weaned from feeding tubes, oxygen, and other special equipment.

The challenges your preemie faces will depend largely on how "old" he was at birth. Babies born between 34 and 37 weeks are considered premature, but usually have few long-term problems. Many of these preemies outgrow their problems and quickly catch up to other children, while "younger" preemies may not catch up until age 3 to 5. In addition, some "younger" preemies exhibit persistent developmental lags. In all, about a third of preemies may face continuing challenges; fortunately, many educational and therapeutic programs are available to help these children not just survive, but thrive.

YOUR PREEMIE'S FIRST FEW MONTHS

When your preemie leaves the hospital and comes home, don't plan on getting much sleep for a while! Preemies, as you've no doubt discovered, have trouble getting to sleep and staying asleep during the night. Even daytime naps and quiet times are tricky, because preemies can easily be overwhelmed by routine sounds, such as a dog barking or a phone ringing. Your preemie is likely to keep you hopping, day and night, at least for a while.

In addition, your preemie will be very sensitive to sights, sounds, touch, and other sensations when she's awake. She may have trouble organizing sensory input at first, and can easily be overwhelmed by her environment. Preemies tend to be easily startled, and are sensitive at the sites where they've had IVs or blood sticks. They also have a hard time dealing with temperature changes, because they aren't as well padded as full-term babies.

You can help keep your preemie calm and relaxed by moving her slowly, and keeping her well supported. When diapering or bathing her, don't make sudden moves or expose her suddenly to changing temperatures; otherwise she may be surprised and scared as her "startle reflex" causes her arms to fly backward. Be careful not to overwhelm your baby with loud noises, lots of visitors, or too many toys. And remember that trips and activities may be more alarming and wearying for her than they would be for a full-term baby. Limit her to one errand or outing per day, until she's able to handle a busier schedule.

You may notice that your baby seems more floppy or is more "stretched out" than full-term babies. That's because she didn't spend as much time curled inside your body. Also, unlike babies who were held snugly by the womb during their final weeks, your baby isn't accustomed to feeling her arms and legs close to her body. In addition, she may seem uncoordinated, and her head may be wobbly.

Your baby will probably outgrow most or all of her problems with time. If you still have concerns by the time she's 2 to 4 months old, ask for a referral to a therapist. Therapy benefits some preemies greatly, while others don't need special intervention.

The exercises and activities that I've included in this section can help calm and comfort your baby, and start her on the road to catching up. Be sure, in particular, to do the positioning exercises. When you position your baby correctly, you'll provide her with some of the sensory experiences that she missed out on by being born early.

One more word of advice, before we get started. No matter how small and fragile your baby seems, develop feelings of confidence when handling her. Babies sense when they're being held firmly and comfortably, and your baby will be more relaxed if she feels secure than if you carry her gingerly and are afraid to touch her. (If you doubt me, watch how the nurses in a hospital obstetrics ward handle preemies.)

Conversely, keep in mind that your baby is more delicate than other infants, and will tire quickly. When exercising or playing with your preemie, quit as soon as she shows signs of fussiness or appears tired. (Often an overstimulated preemie will start hiccuping, look away from you, or become mottled.) If she becomes overstimulated, a slow, rhythmic massage may calm her down. As she grows and matures, she'll be able to handle more and more activity. (And, by the way, she'll start sleeping longer, too—really!)

POSITIONS FOR PREEMIES

Be sure to position your preemie daily. When he lies in the positions shown below, your baby will experience many of the sensations full-term babies experience as they snuggle in Mom's tummy, sucking their thumbs, curling up, and holding their arms and legs close to their bodies.

These positions will help your baby develop more mature muscle tone and stability, and help his body to maintain heat. Positioning will also help your baby develop symmetry, reduce his startle reflex, and teach him how to get comfortable and how to move.

Your baby should spend at least a few minutes each day in each of the positions shown here.

 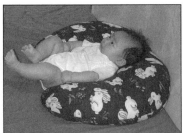

EXERCISE

REST AND RELAX

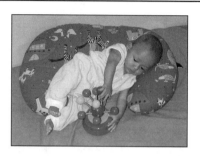

SKILLS TO BUILD

- Tolerance and enjoyment of touch, especially at sites where baby had IVs
- Relaxation and reduction of stress

EQUIPMENT

- Optional: Sleep-A-Bye Cushion or Bop Cushion (available at baby stores)

EXERCISE

- Place your baby on her side in a nested position in the Bop Cushion, on your lap, or in a Sleep-A-Bye Cushion, so she's held firmly and stably.
- Place one hand on your baby's shoulder, and let her grow accustomed to being touched.
- Gently massage the top of your baby's head, stroking back and down. Continue to massage her, moving down her body.
- Watch your baby closely for any signs that she's overstimulated, and slow down or stop until she calms down. Help your baby to relax by massaging her very slowly and quietly at first. As she learns to tolerate the massage, you can talk or sing to her.
- This is a great position to watch baby videos or rest.

PREEMIE TOYS AND TIPS

To help your preemie relax, place him on a bop cushion or a Sleep-A-Bye triangle (available from baby stores), "nesting" him snugly so he feels warm and secure. (Be sure to use baby cushions approved by the Academy of Pediatrics and the SIDS Foundation. Other pillows and cushions can be dangerous.) He'll also enjoy lying in a hammock or a lined pan, which will re-create the feeling of the womb. To enhance this feeling, play womb tapes while he's resting. Also, wrap your baby in a Polar Fleece blanket, a swaddle blanket, or a swaddle coat (available at baby stores), to provide warmth and womblike security.

When you're decorating your premature baby's room, think "simple." Plain, unpatterned blankets, sheets, and walls, in muted colors, will help protect him from overstimulation. Tapes of soft background music, ocean sounds, or "white noise" may help him relax and sleep; introduce these tapes gradually, and keep the volume low. Avoid tapes with both music and singing; the complex auditory input may overwhelm him.

When selecting toys for your preemie, look for toys that provide input to only one sensory system at a time. For instance, avoid colorful mobiles that play music, and instead choose simple toys. Good choices include:

- A mobile with a single shape
- Soft rubber toys that don't make sounds
- Single-color Mylar balloons fastened on your baby's infant seat (do not use balloons without supervision)
- A baby mirror for the crib

One more tip: avoid buying baby walkers or bouncy seats for your preemie. Your baby will benefit more from moving around on the floor than from sitting upright for long periods.

"CAN YOU TELL ME WHY...?"
Answers to Questions Parents of Preemies Often Ask

My husband is afraid to touch our son. They seem to have difficulty bonding. How can I involve Dad and help him become comfortable with our baby?

Let Dad and baby have time together without you. Cuddling in a rocking chair is a wonderful way for them to bond. Also, have your husband walk your baby in the stroller (be sure your stroller is covered, so your baby won't get too much sun and stimulation), or send them out for a drive in the car. At first, your husband may feel less nervous when your baby is safely tucked into a stroller or car seat.

Most parents of preemies, and particularly dads, are somewhat shocked at first by the appearance and fragility of their babies. It's important for both of you to understand that these feelings are normal, and will pass. Don't be too hard on yourselves at first; you've both been through a lot, and you need a little time to adjust and learn to enjoy your baby.

My baby is delayed, but I've been told that she will catch up. How long will it take?

Premature babies may take up to 5 years to fully catch up, although many will be on track by age 2 or 3. Therapy and special-education programs can often help preemies make significant gains.

Remember that your baby's true age is calculated by subtracting the weeks of prematurity from her chronological age. Judge her development using this "corrected" age, rather than comparing her with full-term babies who are the same chronological age.

Special Babies, Special Parents

What experiences did my baby miss by being premature?

If he was born more than 6 weeks early, your baby's respiratory and digestive systems didn't have time to mature fully, so he may need some time to learn to breathe, eat and "poop." Your baby also missed the experience of being bent (flexed) in the womb, which helps a full-term baby learn to suck his thumbs and feet in utero.

Full-term babies fall into their mothers' waking and sleeping patterns during the last 2 months. Because your baby missed this period, his sleep/wake cycle may be out of sync for quite some time.

There wasn't quite enough time for your baby's brain to form all of the pathways usually present by birth, so he has an immature nervous system. It will take some time for him to coordinate sensory input (sights, sounds, movement, touch, taste, smell). As a result, he'll probably have trouble screening out background noise, such as a lawn mower in another yard, and have difficulty tuning out the world when he needs to relax.

My baby seems jittery and shaky. She gets cold very easily, but doesn't like being dressed.

Keep your baby close to you as much as possible. Take naps together, or lie down together when you're watching TV or reading. Listen to soft music or womb tapes together, while you hold her snugly. When you carry her, use a sling carrier. Your baby wasn't ready to be separated from your body as early as she was, and being close to you helps her regain some of the security of the womb.

When you dress your baby, avoid dresses, tights, socks, and shoes. Choose gowns or undershirts with a pull-string or snaps at the bottom, so you can change her diapers without removing her clothing.

What's the best position for my baby to be placed in for sleep?

Place your baby on his back to sleep. Put him on a Prop-A-Bye Cushion, lying on his side to rest or play. This allows him to spit up safely, and the cushion can be adjusted individually to fit your baby's size. It also will hold his body in proper alignment, and prevent him from accidentally rolling over onto his tummy or off the bed. (Note: Do NOT use beanbag cushions or beanbag chairs.)

PREEMIE CHECKLIST—WHEN TO SEEK HELP

 Difficulty using both eyes together

Trouble holding toys

Lack of head control by 4 to 5 months/unable to hold head up and in midline

Difficulty lifting head when on tummy

Rounded back, stiff arms

Arches back, stiff legs, difficulty sitting

Won't take weight on legs

PARENTS' STORIES

JAMAL

Our son Jamal weighed only 2 pounds and 1 ounce when he was born. He was taken straight to the intensive care nursery, and I never even got to hold him. He was so tiny! His hand was no bigger than a thumbnail.

At first, my only concern was for Jamal to stay alive. Every day was another battle to survive, and when Jamal suffered a brain hemorrhage, the doctors were uncertain about his prognosis.

Eventually, however, Jamal turned the corner. He began to gain weight, and his breathing improved. Finally, the nurses let me hold him for a brief but wonderful moment. After another 4 months, he came home to us—along with an apnea monitor and an oxygen tank.

In the hospital, the pediatric therapists had shown us how to support Jamal's tiny body when we fed him or when he rested. After he was released, we still went to therapy sessions twice a week. We celebrated each accomplishment: the first time he lifted his head, the first time he rolled over, the first time he sat up. We had a walking party when he was 18 months old, to celebrate his first independent steps.

Now Jamal is in preschool, and he can count, knows colors, and loves to build with Legos. He's a little more active and impulsive than the other kids, his speech is a bit delayed, and his attention span is somewhat short—but otherwise, he's doing great. Our pediatrician says Jamal may have some learning difficulties later on, but after all we've been through, we're sure we can face any future challenges.

Special Babies, Special Parents

KELLY AND KEVIN

After the nightmare of infertility treatment, we received our reward: we were going to have twins! However, I had bleeding problems throughout my pregnancy, and the babies were born after only 28 weeks.

Kelly was fine, but Kevin had respiratory distress and needed help breathing. He was in the nursery for 6 weeks after Kelly came home. He was soft and wobbly, and was late in learning to hold up his head. He didn't kick his legs the way Kelly did, and he sagged when we stood him up.

When Kevin was 6 months old (4 months in preemie terms, since he arrived 2 months early), our pediatrician referred us to a therapist. She told us Kevin had "hypotonia"—a term meaning low muscle tone—and gave us ideas to help him develop more stability.

We learned to lean Kevin against our shoulders, so he could practice holding his head up without any fear of falling. Also, when I dressed him, I held him over my lap so he could get used to being on his tummy and hold his head up well. We massaged his tummy after each diaper change, which gave him opportunities to practice lifting his legs and bringing both legs together.

We received additional help from a therapist when Kevin was 7 months old and still not sitting. When we put him in a sitting position, he was stiff and hard to bend, and would push backward and fall over. Fortunately, with therapy, he developed more normal muscle tone and learned to sit, crawl, and later to walk.

Kelly walked at 1, while Kevin walked at 2. Since then, however, Kevin has really caught up. We're proud of Kevin for overcoming his rough early start, and pleased to see both of our boys so happy and healthy now.

KEY POINTS FOR PREEMIES

○━⚷ Preemies' nervous systems are immature, and they may be irritable, jittery, and fussy. Swaddling your baby and playing womb tapes can help him relax.

○━⚷ Give your preemie simple toys that stimulate only one sense (for instance, vision or hearing) at a time.

○━⚷ Preemies usually have problems with deep sleep, and don't sleep through the night. They take short naps, and are easily awakened.

○━⚷ All preemies need to be positioned (see "Positions for Preemies"). This helps them experience sensations they missed by leaving the womb early.

○━⚷ Preemies should spend at least 3 minutes a day on their tummies—but only while they're awake, and only with close supervision.

HIGH-NEED BABIES

Most high-need babies don't really belong in a special-needs section, because these babies often outgrow their problems by the age of 6 months or so. However, a small group of them may continue to be extremely fussy, and a very small percentage will have sensory-motor disturbances. By working with your high-need baby early, you can help prevent or minimize future problems—*and* have a calmer, happier baby.

The term "high-need" encompasses a wide range of infants. Some of these babies are slightly premature, have a low birth weight (around 5 to 6 pounds), or were delivered by cesarean section. Others have experienced mild stress before or during birth. At least half, however, are full-term babies with no known birth complications. Oddly, many of these babies are redheads. Also, many are highly intelligent.

What all of these babies have in common is that they're unusually fussy, fearful, and difficult to calm. Many babies are fussy at first (see chapter 1), but high-need babies are far more difficult, for a far longer period, than the average infant.

"HELP—HE'S DRIVING ME NUTS!"

High-need babies are a challenge. They have a very short fuse, and once they're upset, they're very hard to calm. Parents often feel helpless, because no matter how hard they try, nothing seems to work. If you're raising a high-need baby, you'll probably notice that she:

- Has difficulty handling bowel movements and becomes upset when she "poops"
- Is colicky
- Doesn't nurse or feed well

- Dislikes having her diaper changed
- Isn't cuddly
- May have difficulty tolerating going for rides in a car seat or stroller
- Is a very light sleeper, cries when she wakes up, and wakes up frequently at night
- Cries for no identifiable reason, and is often irritable
- Has trouble nursing if she's tired, upset, or very hungry
- Eats for only a few minutes at a time
- Has difficulty using both eyes together to follow objects

Like preemies, high-need babies may have difficulty handling sensory input (sights, sounds, movement, touch, etc.). Thus, they tend to be stressed and fearful when there's too much going on in their environment. Find toys that stimulate only one sense at a time—for instance, toys that move but don't make any noise—and don't let your baby get too tired, hungry, or hot.

Swimming, bathing, and rhythmic activities such as swinging or rocking will help your baby relax. Also, keep her upright after eating, to ease colic.

At least initially, you'll have trouble even with simple activities such as taking a walk on a sunny day. Too much sound, light, and movement bombarding a high-need baby can set off a crying jag that can last for hours. At each change of activity—being changed, dressed, bathed—your baby will be easily upset and hard to calm. You'll probably spend hours walking her, or driving her around in the car, to get her to sleep.

One of the biggest challenges for your high-need baby is sleeping. She may cry herself to sleep, sleep for 20 or 30 minutes, and then wake up crying again. A ringing phone, a barking dog, or even a car horn beeping down the street may wake her up.

Fortunately, most high-need babies settle down after a few months. In the meantime, keep your baby's environment as quiet and relaxing as possible. Also, take care of *yourself*. High-need babies can cause tremendous stress, as well as sleep deprivation that can be harmful to your well-being. So find a good sitter, or enlist your neighbors or relatives to help out, so you can take regular shopping breaks, read a book in the park, or just take a long nap.

Also, be aware that *it's not your fault* you have a fussy, inconsolable baby. Some babies are just born that way, and it has nothing to do with your parenting skills. Don't let well-meaning friends and relatives tell you otherwise!

EXERCISE

Snuggle Up

SKILLS TO BUILD
- Reduced sensitivity to skin-to-skin contact
- Learning the feeling of arms and legs being close to body
- Body awareness
- Accepting and enjoying visual input
- Using both eyes together to focus
- Natural "bending" (flexing)
- Lying on one side

EQUIPMENT
- Small Polar Fleece or receiving blanket for swaddling

EXERCISE
- Place your baby on his back, in the center of the blanket. Gently roll him to his side.
- Let your baby enjoy the feeling of his knees touching each other.

- If needed, bring your baby's top arm and shoulder forward so that his elbows, forearms, and hands are touching.
- Hold your baby firmly so he doesn't fall backward or forward. Swaddle him in the blanket so he's firmly enclosed.
- Lie down and look at your baby without speaking. If he looks away, grimaces, or cries, look away. (Some preemies find eye contact overwhelming at first.)
- Gradually increase your baby's ability to focus and maintain eye contact. As your baby learns to handle stimulation, smile and then hum while doing this exercise. Later, sing to him.

NOTE: No baby should ever be left alone on his tummy, even if swaddled.

HIGH-NEED BABIES: TOYS AND TIPS

What works for preemies also works for high-need babies. The basic rule is: Keep it simple! Buy toys that stimulate only one sense at a time—for instance, rubber toys that don't make noise, mobiles that don't play music, and baby mirrors so your baby can quietly get acquainted with himself. Avoid toys with push buttons that make sounds; instead, look for toys with doors or flaps that reveal pictures or lights.

Your baby may like being swaddled, and may enjoy a hammock or lined oval pan that re-creates the feeling of the womb. (Try lining your baby's stroller with sheepskin, too.) Pick plain, unpatterned sheets and blankets, so you won't overstimulate your baby, and avoid music tapes with both singing and music (select instrumentals instead). If your baby's a fussy eater who's overly sensitive to heat and cold, consider buying a baby bottle with a temperature gauge so you can be sure his formula is just the right temperature.

Many parents report that a special crib insert, called a Rock 'n' Comfort, is a lifesaver. This foam insert moves gently and plays womb music, soothing your baby to sleep. It's available for rental from high-end baby stores, for about $250 for 6 months. Other parents find that the Fisher-Price Soothing Crib Sounds insert calms and comforts their babies.

For parents of high-need babies, a rocking chair is a necessity, not a luxury. Porch swings and battery-operated baby swings also can relax a fussy baby. I recommend light dimmers in baby's room and elsewhere, so that the transition from light to dark (or dark to light) can be gradual rather than sudden. Avoid baby walkers or bouncy seats, which can cause a high-need baby to stiffen.

"CAN YOU TELL ME WHY...?"

Answers to Questions Parents of High-Need
Babies Often Ask

*My husband, relatives, and even my own mother think I'm a
terrible mother because my baby cries all day. Even I feel like
it's my fault. Yesterday, when Michael finally took a nap, I
spent the whole time in the bathroom crying. What am I
doing wrong?*

You're not doing *anything* wrong, except blaming
yourself for something that isn't your fault. Your baby's
difficulties don't stem from inadequate parenting, but
from a nervous system that isn't quite ready to handle
the demands of the world. If your relatives don't believe
you, tell them to read the scientific literature—and tell
them that they'd do you and your baby a lot more good
by pitching in and helping out, rather than criticizing.

If possible, take a break from your baby (and your
relatives) every day. If you can't get a sitter, just put your
baby in his crib, shut the door, and read or watch TV
for a while. Taking care of a high-need baby can be
incredibly stressful, and you need some time off—even
if it's just a few minutes. And hang in there; most high-
need babies become much less difficult starting around
4 months of age.

*My baby cries after each meal, and expecially when she tries
to have bowel movements. She sobs and becomes exhausted.
It's so traumatic for both of us. How can I help her?*

Put your baby on your lap with her legs up against
your chest, and slowly and gently massage her tummy.
This will help her relax and "poop" or pass gas more
easily. Also, keep her upright after meals, in her swing
or on your lap, to help her digest her meals better. If
you're breast-feeding, avoid spicy foods and vegetables

such as broccoli, cabbage, and brussels sprouts, which can upset your baby's tummy. And if you're bottle-feeding, try various types of formula to see if your baby tolerates one better than others.

Also, don't rush to feed your baby solid foods. High-need babies seem more prone to allergies than other babies, and delaying solid foods can help prevent food allergies.

My baby cries whenever I put him down to sleep.

Cribs are scary places for high-need babies. They don't like being alone, with no light and no Mom in sight. If you can, rock your baby to sleep rather than putting him in his crib right away. Wrap him snugly in a blanket, and then, when he's asleep, use the blanket like a crane to move him gently into his crib. Also, develop a routine—for instance, read the same story or sing the same songs before each naptime. Eventually, your baby will associate this routine with "sleepy time." Warm baths make many babies relaxed and drowsy.

I'm breast-feeding, but I don't think my baby is eating enough.

This is a common problem for fussy babies. Often, moms think they're failures if they supplement breast-feeding with bottles, but the best thing you can do for your baby is make sure she's getting enough to satisfy her and keep her healthy. In my experience, 10 to 15 percent of babies need supplemental bottle feedings to really thrive. Try augmenting your breast-feedings with bottle-feedings, and see if your baby becomes happier and healthier.

HIGH-NEED BABY CHECKLIST— WHEN TO SEEK HELP

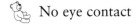 No eye contact

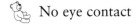 Looking away

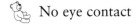 Crying for more than 20–30 minutes

 Always has difficulty with transitions—e.g., crying when waking, going in car, or going outside

 Doesn't like being held

PARENTS' STORIES

SPENCER

Boy, was Spencer ever a challenge! He never slept more than 45 minutes at a time. He wanted to nurse every hour, but he didn't fill out like the fat, round babies in our baby class. I felt so embarrassed when I diapered him in a class, because he'd cry and cry.

By the time Spencer was a few months old, I was exhausted and irritable. I realized that I couldn't be Superwoman, and handle Spencer's constant demands all by myself, so I enlisted my husband's help. He gave Spencer his 2:30 A.M. feeding so I could get some sleep, and he spelled me frequently so I could get out of the house. We did our best to keep our household calm and quiet, and didn't overstimulate Spencer with too many toys or too much loud noise.

Gradually, Spencer fussed less and less. Now, at 1 year of age, he sleeps for 6 hours a night—a huge improvement! He's happy and active, and I think he's as relieved as we are that his fussy baby stage is over.

BRIANNA

I wanted so much to be a mom, but I had no idea what a challenge it would be. Brianna spit up constantly, and I had to change her from head to toe a dozen times a day. She fussed at every feeding and diaper change, and always had a hard time falling asleep. I felt stressed, exhausted, and isolated. Then I went to a moms' support group at a hospital, and found out that I wasn't alone. I met other moms with fussy babies, and we shared ideas and laughs. I also took Brianna to Gymboree, and to a baby swim class. She wasn't an angel on these outings—far from it—but it gave me a chance to get out of the house, meet other people, and regain my sanity. I think those outings, and the moral support I received from my new friends, were what kept me going until Brianna finally outgrew her fussiness and colic.

KEY POINTS FOR THE HIGH-NEED BABY

○━ Like preemies, high-need babies may have difficulty handling sensory input (sights, sounds, movement, touch, etc.). They become stressed and fearful when there's too much going on in their environment.

○━ Try to avoid input to more than one of your baby's senses at a time, because too much input can overwhelm him.

○━ Rocking and swaddling often soothe the high-need baby.

○━ Warm baths may help your baby relax and unwind.

○━ Try to avoid exposure to bright sunlight, and make sure your baby's stroller and car seat are well shaded. Also avoid extreme heat or cold.

○━ Most babies gradually outgrow extreme fussiness as they learn to comfort themselves, sleep better, and tolerate body sensations such as hunger and tiredness.

BABIES WITH ASYMMETRY

The parts of your baby's body work together, like the instruments in an orchestra. And just as an orchestra performs well only if every instrument is in tune, so your baby can sit, stand, or walk well only if all of the parts of his body are working together in symmetry.

If one area of your baby's body is weaker or less developed than the rest, he may have difficulty using that part of his body well. For instance, if one side of his neck is weaker than the other side, his head will tilt to one side, making it hard for him to nurse. If he prefers one hand to the other, he'll have trouble transferring toys from hand to hand, or using his hands together to play or crawl. And if one leg has less muscle tone than the other, he'll have difficulty supporting his weight equally on both legs when he stands.

Asymmetry can make it challenging for a baby to learn skills that require both sides of the body working together. (If one side of your baby's neck is tight or weak, for example, he'll have difficulty keeping his head centered—a skill that's a prerequisite for crawling, sitting, and standing.) Symmetry is also important because your baby needs to use both sides of his body to develop the pathways in both sides of his brain for later learning.

It's important to address asymmetry early on, because your baby is forming sensory patterns that tell him how to move and position his body. If your baby sits with his head tilted for many months, for instance, his brain may say, "This is normal," and he may find normal sitting uncomfortable. In addition, he may develop secondary problems from his asymmetrical positioning, such as muscle shortening or spinal curvature.

Although many cases of asymmetry resolve themselves, some don't—and some asymmetries can be serious. If you have any concerns, it's best to have your baby evaluated by a professional therapist.

Asymmetry has many causes. Some babies experience stress during delivery, as they go through the birth canal. Other babies develop asymmetry in the womb, because of the way they're positioned. Frequently, babies given IVs in one foot or arm may not want to use that body part, or put weight on it. Babies born with a small or partially developed limb may experience some asymmetry. And in some cases, a muscle on one side of the body is simply larger or more developed than the muscle on the other side.

I also see babies whose asymmetry developed because they spent too much time sitting without support, or in jumpers or walkers, before they were ready for this stage. This can cause a baby's back to curve to one side, and can cause actual shortening or deformity.

Asymmetry may affect only your baby's neck, trunk, an arm, or a leg, or it may affect an entire side of his body. With the help of a good therapy program, your baby's asymmetry should improve significantly. By exercising with your baby every day, following a program provided by a professional therapist, you can help equalize the functioning of the two sides of your baby's body. The activities in this section can help your baby make additional progress.

HELPING YOUR BABY GAIN SYMMETRY

Babies who are asymmetrical often turn to one side while eating. It's very important, when bottle-feeding or spoon-feeding an asymmetrical baby, to help your baby look forward and keep his head centered. (It may be necessary to use a head support.) If you're breast-feeding, make sure you breast-feed to both sides equally, even if your baby has a strong preference for one side. If your baby fusses because he doesn't want to nurse on one side, work through this early on—he may give you a hard time for a few days, but eventually he'll give in!

Also, when you're nursing, move your baby's top arm up and forward so it doesn't fall backward.

Your baby may want to play to one side, rather than reaching for toys at the center of his body. If his asymmetry involves his hands, he'll have difficulty grasping and holding toys on one side, and he may keep one hand fisted when playing. He also may find it hard to play with two hands together. Whenever possible, encourage your baby to use his less preferred side. Place toys in his less preferred hand, and position him so that he'll have to use his weaker side to turn and look at you. The more he uses both sides of his body equally, the better off he'll be.

The exercises in this section are meant to supplement your child's therapy plan. They're designed to improve your baby's symmetry, develop his eye-hand coordination, and allow him to experience the feeling of alignment. Try to have your baby play in these positions several times a day, whenever your baby is rested and ready for a workout. You'll be pleased at the progress he'll make!

EXERCISE

Straight Up

SKILLS TO BUILD

- Stability for head, neck, and back muscles
- Sitting up with head centered
- Sensory experience of sitting with head and neck in alignment
- Playing with head in middle, and using eyes and developing optimal eye-hand coordination

EQUIPMENT

- Car seat
- Infant car seat insert
- Infant cloth head support
- Rolled-up towels or foam as needed

EXERCISE

- Place your baby in the seat.
- Provide support as needed, to keep her head centered.
- Support the opposite side of your baby's trunk to keep her back straight.

TIP: Use only an infant car seat for babies up to 20 pounds (versus a larger one that accommodates children up to age 2). The smaller seat provides more support and doesn't need as much padding.

Toys and Tips for Babies Who Exhibit Asymmetry

Toys are wonderful therapy tools for a baby who needs to develop symmetry. To help your baby learn to use her weaker side, give her toys that are lightweight and easy to manipulate. For instance, give her a small inflatable loop to hold in her weaker hand, or purchase the type of jack-in-the-box that's operated by a roller rather than a handle. Easy-to-hold squeak toys, and electronic toys with push buttons, are also excellent choices. Use ponytail holders to attach small toys to your baby's affected limb; this will encourage her to move her arm or leg so she can enjoy the toys.

While you want your baby to use her weaker hand, it's equally important for her to practice using both hands together. Buy her sorting toys, a telephone, a tambourine, pie pans, balls of different sizes, and other toys that require both hands to work together. Finger-painting with whipped cream or "sculpting" with Jell-O will encourage your baby to play with both hands, and allow her to explore new textures.

Sponges will expose your baby to interesting textures, and are easy to hold and release. Also try putting a glove on your baby's weaker hand, to provide texture and focus her attention on that hand. (Or put the glove on her *preferred* hand, so that she'll need to use her other hand to pick up objects.)

If your baby constantly holds her weaker hand fisted, ask her therapist or doctor about using a thumb abduction splint. This device keeps your baby's thumb away from her palm, encouraging her to open her hand.

Bottle covers will catch your baby's attention, and give her extra incentive to practice holding her bottle in both hands. Two-handled cups also will help her learn to use both hands together.

"CAN YOU TELL ME WHY...?"
Answers to Questions Often Asked by Parents of Babies Who Exhibit Asymmetry

My 6-month-old baby's left hand just lies by his side. He uses his right hand a lot. What can we do to help him use his left hand?

If your baby's hand is fisted, he may have difficulty learning to use his fingers. To help him relax and open his hand, frequently place your hand inside his in a handshake position. Also, fill a dishpan with lentils or water and encourage your baby to scoop it with his hand, keeping his thumb up. And give him "two-handed" toys, such as large stuffed toys, pie pans, cloth books, and balls too large to hold with one hand.

Play hand-in-hand games such as push-pull, in which you push with your open hand against your baby's hand, while supporting his arm at the elbow and keeping it forward. It's important to let your baby experience the feeling of weight on his open hand.

My baby holds her bottle only with her right hand. Is this okay?

Your baby needs to use both hands. Buy a bottle cover to make it easier and more fun for her to hold her bottle, and help her bring her left arm forward to hold the bottle. When you play with her, kiss her left hand, and encourage her to touch your face with that hand. During bath time, encourage her to splash the water with her left hand.

My baby's head always falls to the left side. How can I correct this?

Keep your baby's head propped in alignment, using

rolled towels and/or a commercially available head support—especially when he's in his car seat or infant seat. Also, see the exercises in chapter 2.

ASYMMETRICAL BABY CHECKLIST—
WHEN TO SEEK HELP

- Trouble using both eyes together to look at and follow objects

- Head falls to one side—baby does not hold head centered

- Looks only one way

- Bats at toys using only one side

- Rolls only one way

- Tight-fisted hands past 3 months

- More movement in arms than in legs

- Doesn't reach for feet or knees by 6 months

- Constantly fisted hand and stiff leg on one side

PARENTS' STORIES

AUSTIN

Austin's head always fell to the left. It was hard even to wash his neck on the left side, because there was so little space between his ear and shoulder.

At his 6-week checkup, the nurse suggested that we use a head support and a rolled-up towel to center Austin's head. At his 3-month checkup, however, his head still tilted to the left. The doctor said that Austin might outgrow this on his own, but my husband and I wanted to consult a therapist.

After a thorough evaluation, the therapist said Austin was on target developmentally. However, she said he had a slight muscle imbalance. She gave us tips on how to position Austin's head correctly, and taught us exercises to help equalize the muscle tone on the two sides of Austin's neck. Now he holds his head up perfectly in midline. We aren't worried about his development anymore—and it's a lot easier to wash his neck!

EVAN

As a baby, Evan suffered a subdural hematoma (bleeding inside his brain). Afterward, we noticed that he had lots of trouble using his left side. Our doctor suggested that Evan could benefit from therapy.

The therapist showed us how to present each toy or activity to Evan's weaker side. Initially Evan fussed a little, but slowly and gradually he learned to open his left hand while playing. We helped him practice dropping toys with his left hand, and he learned to sit on his left side, look to his left, and stand with his right leg up so all of his weight was on his left side. He was a late walker, because it took him time to develop coordination on his left side—but we were so excited when he learned to walk while pushing a big ball to support himself. Now he walks everywhere, and his left side lags a little only when he's tired.

KEY POINTS FOR BABIES WHO EXHIBIT ASYMMETRY

☞ The parts of your baby's body work together, like the instruments in an orchestra. Your baby can sit, stand, or walk well only if all of the parts of his body function together in symmetry.

☞ By doing exercises to improve your baby's symmetry, you'll help him create sensory-motor patterns that will enable him to use his body correctly. Improving your baby's symmetry also will help prevent long-term problems such as abnormal neck or spine curvature, or pain.

☞ To help overcome symmetry problems, encourage your baby to use his less-preferred side or body part regularly. Encourage him to use both sides of his body when he eats and plays.

☞ It's important to address asymmetry early on. Otherwise, your baby may grow accustomed to using his body asymmetrically, and feel uncomfortable when he's positioned correctly.

☞ Asymmetry usually begins at the head, so be sure to keep your baby's head centered!

BABIES WITH LOW MUSCLE TONE

Picture your baby's muscles as rubber bands. If your baby has low muscle tone, the rubber bands are too loose, and don't work efficiently. Your baby may seem soft and overly flexible, a little like a rag doll, and you may find that it's hard to hold her without her slipping right through your arms.

Your baby may have difficulty lifting her head or lifting her legs to kick, and she may not like being on her tummy because it's hard for her to push up on her arms. When she learns to sit, her back may be rounded. She may be slow to sit, stand, and walk, but most babies with low muscle tone master these skills with a little help and lots of encouragement—so be patient!

Babies with low muscle tone (hypotonia) generally have unstable, overly flexible hip, shoulder, elbow, and knee joints. They tend to lie with their legs spread wide and turned out at the knees, and when they stand, their knees may bend slightly backward and their feet may roll in over their ankles. Low-tone babies also have slow reflexes, so it's often hard for them to protect themselves with their arms when they lose their balance. Some low-tone babies have normal tone in their small muscles, and have little or no trouble using their fingers and hands well.

In most cases, low tone will improve as babies grow. In fact, some low-tone babies become good gymnasts, because they're so flexible! A relatively small number of babies have persistent low tone, but therapy and exercise can improve their strength and stability, refine their protective reactions so they can catch themselves if they lose their balance, and reduce delays in achieving milestones such as sitting and walking. As their muscle tone improves, it will be easier and more enjoyable for these babies to move and explore their world.

USE THOSE MUSCLES!

If your baby has low muscle tone, she needs to play on her tummy as much as possible. This will allow her to develop her neck, back, and arm muscles by pulling up against gravity. It also will help her develop the skills needed for protective extension—the reaction in which her arms move forward or sideways to catch her if she falls when sitting. She'll need good protective extension to sit up well later, and to protect her head if she loses her balance. Tummy play helps your baby practice all three elements of protective extension: positioning her arms, taking weight on her arms, and moving her arms quickly.

If your baby is uncomfortable playing on her tummy, put a rolled-up towel under her chest, or place her on her tummy over your lap. She won't like playing on her tummy as much as she likes playing on her side, where she doesn't have to fight gravity, and she may fuss at first. Work for short periods, give her interesting toys to watch, and act happy and excited so she'll think you're both having fun. If you're lucky, you'll fool her!

It's also *very* important for your baby to stand with support by the time she's 5 or 6 months old. When she stands, your baby will be resisting gravity, an action that improves muscle tone and helps her develop a strong, straight back. Supported standing also helps your baby's hip sockets form correctly, and builds endurance, symmetry, and strength. In addition, it helps stabilize her back, leg, and hip joints.

One more note about standing: The baby with low tone is an exception to the "barefoot is better" rule. Your baby needs extra support, so buy her old-fashioned, high-top, lace-up shoes.

"Nesting" can help your low-tone baby by stabilizing her large joints so that it's easier for her to move. Place your baby in a tub, large bowl, laundry basket, or cardboard box, padded with towels or blankets that snugly support her back, hips, and shoulders and keep her legs together. (Give her wrist and foot rattles to enjoy while she's "nesting.")

Avoid using thick cloth diapers if your baby has low muscle tone, because they keep your baby's legs too widely separated. Also, dress your baby in lightweight clothes whenever possible. Babies with low muscle tone have a hard time moving when they're dressed in heavy, bulky pants or sweaters.

Brisk, firm massages of your baby's legs, feet, and tummy are helpful, because they help her muscles "wake up" and work better. Even if you don't have time for exercises, work in a daily tummy massage; this simple activity will tone your baby's abdominal muscles and encourage her to lift her legs up to her chest, helping her integrate the top and bottom parts of her body.

Low-tone babies tend to be easygoing and placid, and your baby may need some encouragement to get started on the exercises and activities in this section. She probably likes sitting or lying quietly and watching the world go by, so it's up to you to motivate her with lots of praise and an excited

This carrying position should **not** be used with a low-tone baby because it does not keep baby's legs together

attitude. (Think Richard Simmons!) On the bright side, low-tone babies usually are more cheerful and cooperative than other babies, and generally they have a ball once they start moving. Try exercising to perky music with a good beat, in order to pick up your baby's pace. Start out by picking her up and dancing with her. When she feels you moving, it will encourage her to get moving herself.

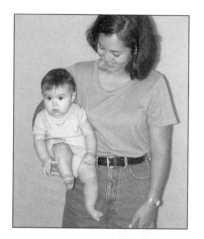

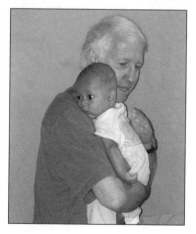

These are the best positions for carrying a low-tone baby. In the bottom position, if your baby's arms are down (as shown), bring them up against your chest to help baby practice holding her head up and taking weight on her shoulders.

EXERCISE

Legs Together

SKILLS TO BUILD
- Experiencing sensory feeling of having legs and knees touching
- Bringing both legs together
- Sleeping with legs together
- Preventing leg muscles from being overstretched
- Encouraging leg and hip development

EQUIPMENT
- Drawstring gown or blanket bag sleeper fairly close to baby's size, so that it fits closely but is *not* tight

EXERCISE
- Dress your baby in the gown or sleeper—put legs in first.
- Place your baby's legs together inside the gown or sleeper.
- Place your baby on his side or back.
- Encourage your baby to play in this position.

NOTE: When your baby is in his car seat or infant seat, place rolled-up small towels to the sides of his legs to hold his legs together.

TOYS AND TIPS FOR BABIES
WITH LOW MUSCLE TONE

Most babies with low tone are almost impossible to over-stimulate, so go for toys that make noise, create bright patterns, and have interesting textures. Hang up colorful pictures and mobiles in your baby's room, too, and buy her brightly patterned sheets and blankets. She'll enjoy tapes of children's music, and musical rattles or bells.

Also buy your baby toys that tempt her to lift her arms and legs, because moving her body against gravity will improve her muscle tone. Wrist rattles, foot rattles, bracelets, bright socks, and hand puppets are fun, and will give her a good workout. (You also can paint her toenails a bright color, or color her toes with washable, nontoxic food coloring.) A Baby Gym will improve tone in her arms and tummy, and help her develop balance reactions that will prepare her for crawling and walking. So will playing "This Little Piggy" on her fingers or toes.

If your baby has trouble grasping and holding toys, buy her small, thin, lightweight toys, about 2 to 3 inches in size, that are easy to grab and lift. (Good choices include a rubber dog, a Swiss rattle, foam keys and toys, small fabric dolls, cloth or lightweight plastic books, and inflatable toys.) Keep her toys close to her, so she can reach them easily. When she's old enough, buy your baby toys that can be pushed. When she pushes a toy, she'll be working against resistance, which builds muscle tone and strength.

Be sure your low-tone baby spends time in a baby swing, or that you rock her in a rocking chair or on a porch swing. Swinging is good exercise for a low-tone baby, and actually helps stimulate the development of brain pathways. Make sure to adjust the seat so that your baby's legs are together, and use rolled washcloths at either side to provide stability if needed.

Musical toys and toys with moving patterns will help keep your baby occupied while she's playing on her tummy. If she has vision problems, give her bright toys that are easy to see. You also can entertain her during "tummy play" by placing her on a bright, textured quilt or a musical quilt.

Decorated cloth bottle covers will encourage your baby to lift her arms to hold her bottle independently. When she's ready to drink from a cup, buy her a two-handled cup that's easy to hold.

"CAN YOU TELL ME WHY...?"

Answers to Questions Parents of Babies with Low Muscle Tone Often Ask

My baby is such a good baby, but he doesn't move very much. He stays wherever I place him, and seems lazy. Is this common in babies with low muscle tone?

Yes, because moving is hard work for a baby with low tone—and muscles are heavy! At first, your baby may need lots of praise, encouragement, and help to get him moving. But it'll get easier with time, just as it does when *you* exercise. Exercise for short periods, and provide lots of repetition.

It's very important, also, not to let your baby become passive. Don't make life too easy for him; challenge him to be active, and to initiate play and other activities.

My baby feels "loosey-goosey" when I dress her, as though she's going to slip through my fingers. I have to keep my hands all over her body to support her.

Babies with low tone are hard to hang on to, because they lack stability and the ability to hold a position. Your baby will gradually learn to stabilize herself; in the meantime, be sure to get a good grip on her when you pick her up. *Never* pull her up by her arms or pull on her legs. She needs to have her large joints well supported.

Does "low muscle tone" mean that my baby's muscles are weak?

Many parents are surprised to learn that low muscle tone usually *doesn't* stem from a disorder of the muscles themselves. Rather, the messages *to* the muscles, telling them to initiate movement, are insufficient. Most of the time, the muscles themselves are perfectly normal.

My baby is 10 months old and won't put any weight on his feet. This could be a sensory problem. Try the "Brush My Feet" exercise (see chapter 8), or apply pressure to one foot by pushing it against a mirror or wall. To make this more fun, place a bright sticker or picture on the mirror or the wall, and have your baby touch it with one foot at a time. Also, when you change your baby, bring his legs together and let him push his feet against the floor or changing table. Be sure his feet and legs are in good alignment.

My baby weighed 8½ pounds when she was born, but now she's getting pudgy. Is this common for babies with low tone? Yes—in part because they don't move as much as other babies, so they aren't burning as many calories. As your baby gets older, extra weight will make it harder for her to move, so be sure not to overfeed her. However, many low-tone babies put on extra pounds even if they don't eat excessively.

Keep your baby on the floor as much as possible, because she'll get more of a workout during floor play than she will when she's sitting in an infant seat. Also, she'll benefit from structured, regular exercise.

LOW-TONE BABY CHECKLIST— WHEN TO SEEK HELP

🐨 Floppy head

🐨 Trouble holding head centered in midline

🐨 Difficulty lifting head when on tummy or pushing up on arms

🐨 Doesn't move much

🐨 Difficulty taking weight when standing; sags

🐨 Stiff legs

🐨 Pushing back with head

🐨 Trouble sitting alone, poor balance

🐨 Floppy, with intermittent stiffness, trouble bending

PARENTS' STORIES

KRISTIN

Kristin's arms and legs were widely spread, and the nurse in the doctor's office said she had hypotonia. To improve her muscle tone, we massaged her tummy during each diaper change. We'd also kiss her tummy and make "raspberries" on her belly button, to make her lift her legs. Gradually she started moving more and more, and we could tell that the muscle tone in her legs was improving. At her 9-month exam, she kicked the doctor's dangling stethoscope! Now she loves gymnastics, and she runs, jumps, and even does somersaults.

NICK

Nick couldn't get into a sitting position. To get down to the floor, he'd just spread his legs wide and fall forward to the floor, doing a "split." His therapist taught him to reach across the middle of his body to get toys, and to come up to a sitting position while moving a toy. When we diapered him, we'd bring him up partway in a half-circle, and let him come up the rest of the way. After lots of practice, he learned to get into a sitting position with ease—and boy, did his upper arms get stronger. Now he can throw a ball all the way across the room!

KEY POINTS FOR THE BABY
WITH LOW MUSCLE TONE

☞ "Tummy time" is critical for the baby with low tone. When he's on his tummy, your baby develops his neck, back, and arm muscles, and improves the protective reflexes that help protect him from head injury if he falls while sitting, standing, or walking.

☞ Daily gentle tummy massages after a diaper change will tone your baby's tummy muscles, and help him integrate the top and bottom of his body.

☞ In general, don't worry about overstimulating a baby with low tone! Buy him colorful, noisy toys. Also buy toys that encourage him to lift his arms and legs, because moving his body against gravity improves his muscle tone. Lightweight toys are good for babies who have difficulty grasping.

☞ The baby with low tone needs sturdy, high-top shoes that provide foot and ankle support.

☞ It's easy to let your baby be passive, but he'll be better off if you encourage him to move! Daily play activities will help him develop muscle tone and stability.

BABIES WITH DELAYED DEVELOPMENT

When I think of developmentally delayed babies, I'm always reminded of the wonderful essay "Welcome to Holland," by Emily Perl Kingsley. Kingsley compares the experience of parenting a developmentally delayed child to the experience of planning a trip to Italy, only to find out you've been sidetracked to Holland. It's not a terrible place, she says, "just a different place . . . [and] after you've been there for a while and you catch your breath, you look around . . . and you begin to notice that Holland has windmills . . . and Holland has tulips. Holland even has Rembrandts."

That's how it is when you learn that your child is developmentally delayed. At first, you're shocked. But soon you discover that your baby is a delight, and that "different" isn't bad. I can pretty much guarantee, from my decades of experience with special babies and their parents, that you'll get every bit as much joy from your developmentally delayed baby as you would from any other child.

That doesn't mean, however, that you won't face challenges—especially when your baby is very young. But with the help of a good special-education program, therapy, and lots of hard work, you'll overcome them together.

WHAT DOES "DEVELOPMENTALLY DELAYED" MEAN?

"Developmentally delayed" is a broad category, and it includes lots of different infants. Some of them will catch up to their peers, while others will remain delayed. But don't be too quick to develop preconceived notions about what your baby can or can't achieve. Two of my patients with Down's syndrome have graduated from junior college, and are almost fully independent. While a number of adults with developmental delays don't function at that level, most are out in the community, working, playing, going to school, and leading happy and fulfilling lives.

It's likely that no one, even your baby's doctor, can predict what your baby will be able to accomplish when she grows up. Whatever her potential, however, you can maximize her progress by seeking out early intervention programs through your school district, your local children's hospital, or organizations that work with developmentally delayed children.

WHAT TO EXPECT:
SOME COMMON FEATURES OF
DEVELOPMENTAL DELAY

It's important to throw out the standard developmental charts if you have a developmentally delayed baby, because your baby will grow and learn at her own rate. She'll be slower in motor skills such as sitting and walking, and it will probably taker her longer to develop speech and play skills. Some developmentally delayed babies are uniformly slow, while others have islands of skills and areas of extreme delay.

Your baby may have trouble breast-feeding and may sleep a lot. Foods with texture may make her gag, and she may like only a few foods. She'll probably stay at the oral stage longer than most babies, and will still like to chew on toys or her fingers when she's 6 months or a year old (or even older). She may have difficulty with oral motor skills, such as keeping her tongue in her mouth, and she may drool a great deal, but these problems can be lessened by therapy.

Many babies who are slower are cuddly and social and enjoy people. Sometimes they'll sit happily in the same place for hours. Your baby may be one of these "easy" and undemanding types, especially if she has Down's syndrome.

Other delayed babies, however, tend to be stubborn. Some also are oversensitive, and have trouble making eye contact.

If your baby is easily overstimulated or shies away from contact with people, present new sights, sounds, and people very gradually. Work to develop eye contact and visual attention; one good technique is to lean close to your child, firmly say "Look at me," and make a "v" with your fingers while pointing them toward your eyes. And don't take it personally if your baby avoids looking at you. Difficulty in making eye contact can stem from visual or sensory problems; it *doesn't* mean that your baby is rejecting you. Reward your baby for looking at you, with a suck on her bottle or a toy.

Your baby may have trouble integrating and understanding movement, sound, colors, and faces. To overcome these problems, she'll need to work on tracking objects with her eyes, locating and "fixing" on sounds or sights, and connecting sights to related sounds (for instance, understanding that her kitty is making the "meowing" sound).

When working with your baby, remember that she'll need lots of repetition. Often, after the tenth or hundredth time, you'll see the light dawn in her eyes, as if she's saying, "Oh—I get it!" Be patient, and offer lots of reinforcement. Praise any attempts at first, then gradually shape your baby's responses by offering more enthusiastic praise when her responses are closest to the one you're working toward. Be sure to keep your directions simple (one or two words). Above all, let her progress at her own pace!

The following activities will help your baby learn to play, explore her world, and develop her cognitive skills. Because no two special babies are alike, you may want to check the other sections in this chapter for exercises and activities that will benefit your child. (In particular, many babies with developmental delays have low muscle tone—see previous section.) If your baby is in a therapy program, ask the therapist which exercises will be most helpful.

EXERCISE

Tummy Time

SKILLS TO BUILD

- Playing on tummy
- Developing eye-hand coordination
- Exploring balance and weight-shifting safely
- Improving arm/shoulder strength
- Using hands and fingers to develop fine motor coordination skills

EQUIPMENT

- Well-padded surface
- Brightly colored activity quilt (quilt with soft toys attached, bright shapes, patterns, and faces, soft baby mirror)

EXERCISE

- Place your baby on the floor, facedown, and stand or lie next to or behind her. Place one hand under her tummy and lift her so her arms are forward. Use your other hand to push down on your baby's arms. Be sure your baby's elbows are in line with her shoulders, and her hands are forward.

- Encourage your baby to reach forward and touch an interesting part of the quilt.
- If your baby fusses, provide support to her tummy or use a small, rolled-up towel.
- Always supervise your baby when she's on her tummy, to make sure her airway is clear and she doesn't fall asleep.
- If your baby is tired, turn her over onto her back.
- Place your baby over your lap at an incline if she fusses when on her tummy on the floor.

TOYS AND TIPS FOR THE BABY
WITH DEVELOPMENTAL DELAY

Babies with developmental delays like toys that are easy to operate—for instance, books with push buttons, or toys with large switches. Musical toys that create moving pictures or patterns also are good choices, because they stimulate several of your baby's senses at once.

Blow bubbles for your baby; he'll enjoy watching them float in the air, and watching them will improve his "eye tracking" skills. (If you get tired of this activity before he does, use a fan to blow the bubbles for you.) Also let him "finger paint" with Jell-O, whipped cream, or yogurt. He'll have fun, and he'll get some good arm and hand exercise at the same time.

It's important for your baby to move, so buy a baby swing or rocking chair. Your baby should spend at least half an hour each day swinging or being rocked. Also, sitting in an inflatable inner tube or lying on an inflatable mattress will give your baby a good workout and improve his balance skills. (But never leave him alone in the tube or on the mattress.) To make an inexpensive and educational toy, put plastic balls (available from toy stores) in a big cardboard box and string toys across the top; again, always supervise your baby while he's enjoying this play activity.

Soft, light rubber toys are good for babies who have difficulty grasping objects. For "tummy time," place your baby on a quilt with different textures (corduroy, satin, etc.), to provide sensory input and keep him interested while he's working out. To teach your baby "object permanence"—the understanding that people and objects still exist even when they aren't in sight—give him a small doll with a blanket attached. Play peek-a-boo, using the blanket to hide the doll.

If your baby doesn't seem interested in a toy at first, don't give up. Show him how to use the toy, by placing your hand over his and helping him push buttons or flip switches. Keep practicing, and your baby's likely to decide, after some consideration, that he *loves* his new toy!

"CAN YOU TELL ME WHY...?"
Answers to Questions Parents of Babies with Developmental Delays Often Ask

I feel overwhelmed by all of the doctor's appointments, therapy visits, and insurance paperwork I have to deal with. Is this what my life will be like from now on?

You're not alone if you're feeling stressed. A common saying among parents of special-needs babies is "It's not your baby who will drive you crazy. It's the system!" The first few years of raising a special-needs baby are usually the most hectic, and it may often seem as though your baby has become a diagnosis rather than a child. The good news is that life generally calms down when a developmentally delayed baby reaches preschool age.

In the meantime, it's important to realize that you can't be SuperMom every day. Set priorities, and don't feel guilty if you occasionally take a day off. Also, enlist your friends and family members to help out by taking your baby to therapy sessions. If your child is a client of your state's Department of Developmental Disabilities, see if her case manager can help you with paperwork. (Your insurance company should be able to help, too.) Talk to the staff in your doctor's billing office, and see if they can offer assistance.

Most important, remember that your baby isn't a disability. She's a wonderful, unique, growing, learning little person with special gifts as well as special needs. Take time to enjoy her, and be proud of her—and be proud of yourself, for the help you're giving her.

We're transitioning our baby from a feeding tube to independent feeding, but he's not eating much on his own. What can we do?

Your doctor can refer you to a feeding therapist.
Also, try these activities:

- Encourage your baby to suck his fingers. This will develop his mouth muscles, and help him get used to the sensation of having something in his mouth. This may be uncomfortable for your baby at first, but don't give up; have him practice thumb-sucking twice a day, and he'll probably start to enjoy this activity.
- Put soft rubber toys in your baby's mouth (be sure they're too big to swallow), and encourage him to suck and chew on the toys. This will improve his feeding skills now, and improve his speech skills later.
- Do "tongue walks," pushing down on your baby's tongue with your finger at quarter-inch intervals from the tip to the center of the tongue. Also, pat and stroke his cheeks.
- If your baby is at least 4 months old, ask his doctor if it's okay to start feeding him thickened cereal.
- Practice giving your baby tiny amounts of liquid with a spoon. Push down on his tongue and let the spoon rest on his lower lip. Wait until he uses his upper lip to take the food off the spoon. (Do this exercise only after checking with your doctor.)

My doctor says my baby can start an infant development class when she's only 6 months old. Isn't this too early? Am I pushing her too hard?

We've learned in recent years that early intervention plays a critical role in helping babies with developmental delays achieve their full potential. Don't worry about pushing your baby if you enroll her in a program at an early age, because teachers and therapists working with babies know how to make their programs entertaining. You'll probably be surprised at how much fun your baby has!

Enrolling your baby in therapy or a special-education program will also benefit *you*, by introducing you to other parents facing the same challenges you're facing. You'll be able to share ideas, concerns, and (if you're lucky) even baby-sitters, and you're likely to make some lifelong friends.

DEVELOPMENTALLY DELAYED BABY CHECKLIST—WHEN TO SEEK HELP

 Slow to sit

Slow to hold head up

Slow to respond to sound

Can't play on his own

Slow to/can't imitate by 10 months of age gestures such as lip-smacking, patting, "Ooo" vowel sounds, smiling

Almost always mouths objects versus playing with them

Doesn't move, won't go after toy

Moves very slowly

Few varied vocalizations

Appears uninterested in playing with toys

Appears uninterested in other people

PARENTS' STORIES

MOLLY

We were shocked when an amniocentesis revealed that our baby had Down's syndrome. Molly was born with a heart defect that required surgery, and she had to be tube-fed for a long time and couldn't swallow liquids.

Molly's therapists taught her to suck and swallow, and showed us exercises to develop her oral motor skills. They placed special emphasis on pushing down on her tongue every time she stuck it out. It was hard work, but we could see the results. She doesn't drool at all now, and she keeps her mouth and lips closed, with her tongue well inside her mouth. Thanks to therapy, she has a beautiful smile.

Now, at 3¹/₂, Molly is a beautiful blonde with bright blue eyes who walks, runs, knows her colors, and loves books and Barney. At preschool, she greets everyone with a hug and a big "Hi." We didn't know how much fun, joy, and growth Molly would bring into our lives. We're certainly grateful that she's ours!

SAM

We didn't know there was anything wrong with Sam until she was a year old. That's when we started worrying, because she didn't learn to talk and couldn't walk. The doctors kept telling us, "She'll catch up," but she didn't. Finally we had her evaluated at a local medical center, where we learned that she had a chromosome abnormality. She didn't learn to walk until she was nearly 2 years old, and she knew only 2 or 3 words.

Luckily, we found a wonderful school for Sam when she was 2. The therapists there taught her to stand and walk bet-

ter, and eventually she learned to walk on a balance beam, ride a 3-wheeled bike, roller-skate, and swing by herself. The therapy also stimulated her to talk more, and her new abilities really opened up her world.

KEY POINTS FOR CHILDREN WITH DEVELOPMENTAL DISABILITIES

- With education, therapy, and lots of help from their parents, babies with developmental delays can make remarkable strides. Their development is slower, but they *can* learn—often more than you expect!

- When teaching your baby new skills, use plenty of repetition. Be positive and animated. Plan regular, structured activities, rather than waiting for your baby to initiate activities.

- Babies with developmental delays enjoy toys that are easy to operate—for instance, toys with push buttons or big switches. Musical toys also are good choices. These babies tend to love music, and often learn and exercise best with background music.

- Encourage your baby to move. He'll enjoy swinging and rocking, and these activities will help build brain pathways.

- Like all babies, babies with developmental delays benefit from structure and praise. They also benefit from being challenged to reach their full potential, so don't give in on everything. Give your baby a little push occasionally, and see how far he'll go!

A WORD ABOUT PEDIATRIC THERAPY

If your baby has any significant physical problems, you'll probably be referred to a pediatric therapist. Early therapy can help your baby catch up before important developmental stages are missed. Most babies enjoy therapy sessions, which are filled with interesting activities designed to match their interests and abilities.

BABIES WHO MAY NEED EARLY HELP

HEALTH ISSUES
- Complications during delivery
- Prematurity
- Small for gestational age
- Failure to thrive/poor weight gain
- Intracranial bleeding
- Heart surgery

DEVELOPMENTAL ISSUES
- Slow development
- Chromosomal or genetic syndrome

ORTHOPEDIC NEEDS
- Spina bifida
- Torticollis
- Seizures
- Asymmetry

NEUROLOGICAL ISSUES
- Head injury
- Seizures
- Atypical muscle tone
- Muscle weakness

Special Babies, Special Parents

Some babies are referred for therapy almost immediately after discharge from the hospital, and many others are referred sometime during the first year of life. With cutbacks in health care and the advent of managed care, access to services is sometimes very limited. You may have to fight to get services, but it will be worth the effort. With early intervention and a home program, your baby will be able to attain his full potential.

Usually after each therapy session you'll be given homework to do with your baby. It may include ways to dress, feed, and play with your baby in certain positions. Be sure to follow through, because the extra time you spend can greatly enhance your child's progress. Grandparents, baby-sitters, and older siblings can be active participants in your baby's therapy. Far from being stressful or difficult, therapy time can be an entertaining experience full of smiles, giggles, and memorable moments.

Be sure to find a therapist you like and feel comfortable with. Don't hesitate to shop around, and be just as picky as you'd be in choosing a pediatrician or physician. Also, look for a therapist who wants you to be a full partner in your child's therapy, not just an onlooker.

Once you get started, stick with it—even if some sessions are tedious or frustrating. One thing I've learned, in more than 20 years of working with "special" babies, is that they can accomplish amazing things. Whether it's sitting up without support, saying a word, picking up a spoon, or taking a first step, each of your baby's achievements will more than repay your hard work!

Afterword

I hope you've enjoyed the exercises and activities in this book, and I hope that as your baby grows up, you'll continue to "work out" together. As your child grows and matures, you'll find a wealth of activities—from ball games to swimming—that you can enjoy as a family. These are wonderful ways for you and your child to build a strong relationship.

In addition to working out with your child, make time every day to read or play together. Enriching your child's environment can be as easy as sharing a game of blocks, enjoying a bedtime reading ritual, or even playing with water in the sink. No matter how hectic your work schedule is, be sure to schedule in "together time" with your son or daughter. Childhood goes by quickly, and it's important to treasure your moments together. When you share fun activities, you'll help strengthen not only your child's mind and body but also your family ties. In addition, you'll create wonderful memories that will last a lifetime!